Stephen Hawking, "A Brief History of Time"
Fred Allen Wolf, "Star Wave"
Michael Talbot, "Mysticism & the New Physics"

EXPLORING INNER AND OUTER SPACE

EXPLORING INNER AND OUTER SPACE

A Scientist's Perspective on Personal and Planetary Transformation

BRIAN O'LEARY, Ph.D.

North Atlantic Books, Berkeley, California

Exploring Inner and Outer Space: A Scientists's Perspective on Personal and Planetary Transformation

ISBN 1–55643–068–X paperback
1–55643–069–8 cloth

Published by North Atlantic Books
2800 Woolsey Street
Berkeley, California 94705

Cover photograph of the Gulf of Mexico courtesy of NASA
Cover and book design by Paula Morrison
Typeset by Campaigne and Somit Typography

Dr. O'Leary is available to give lectures and seminars on this subject. For more information, write to him at Future Focus, 5136 East Karen Drive, Scottsdale, Arizona 85254.

Exploring Inner and Outer Space: A Scientist's Perspective on Personal and Planetary Transformation is sponsored by the Society for the Study of Native Arts and Sciences, a nonprofit educational corporation whose goals are to develop an ecological and crosscultural perspective linking various scientific, social, and artistic fields; to nurture a holistic view of arts, sciences, humanities, and healing; and to publish and distribute literature on the relationship of body, mind, and nature.

Library of Congress Cataloging-in-Publication Data

O'Leary, Brian, 1940–
Exploring inner and outer space: a scientist's perspective on personal and planetary transformation / by Brian O'Leary.
p. cm.
Includes bibliographical references.
ISBN 1–55643–069–8 : $25.00
ISBN 1–55643–068–X (pbk.) : $12.95
1. Outer space—Exploration. 2. Parapsychology and science. I. Title.
TL793.044 1989
133—dc20 89–22972
CIP

To the Higher Power who guides us all
from our inner and outer space and
To all of us who are growing in awareness of our
immortality and our multidimensional being.

ACKNOWLEDGEMENTS

Laurene Johnson, my significant other, sacrificed hours of her time to comment on my first draft and tolerated my intensity over a period of three months. I deeply appreciate her patience. I also thank the following individuals for freely contributing their insights, time, honesty and other assistance during this project: Cleve Backster, Nancy Busnack, Mark Carlotto, Frank Chilton, Tina Choate, Dan Drasin, Richard Grossinger, Obadiah Harris, Stuart and Judy Heywood, Jon Klimo, Judy Miller, Brian Myers, Fred O'Leary, Marilyn Powers, Andrija Puharich, Julie Roache, John and Marilyn Rossner, Whitley and Anne Strieber, Maralyn Teare, Frank White and Steve White.

I am also grateful to John-Roger and Arnold Patent, whose teachings have stirred within me a deep sense of cosmic awareness that has transcended my training as a scientist. I have often wanted to present in this book their expression of universal principles that are similar to those I am proposing based on my own experience and scientific results. I have not done so only because I have wanted to stay as close to the scientific approach as possible.

CONTENTS

PUBLISHER'S FOREWORD

The 1970s movie *Capricorn One* opens with a rocket ship in its gantry—the first manned spaceflight to Mars hours from launch. As the countdown proceeds, we witness a behind-the-scenes dilemma of beleagured NASA officials trying to hold onto their dwindling share of government funds. As the final seconds are counted off, three startled astronauts are suddenly removed from the capsule, helicoptered to a jet, and then flown to a deserted army base three hundred miles outside of Houston. The countdown continues and the rocket is fired. As far as the world, and most of the employees of NASA, are concerned, these men are on their way to Mars. The world will continue to believe this for the duration of the flight.

This deception was provoked by a late-discovered flaw in the ship's life-support system. In the words of the project director, "[A contractor] made a little bit too much profit. You guys would all be dead in three weeks." Yet, cancellation would also spell doom for NASA, so they must pretend to go to Mars.

The crew, captained by a man named Brubaker (James Brolin), is blackmailed into collaboration by a mortal threat to their wives and children. For almost a year the men are held under guard by a CIA-like agency and used, when appropriate, for mock broadcasts from space and from Mars. The apparent plan is to have the capsule land off target at sea, giving NASA time to put them back in. By then presumably, they will be accomplices and in no position to reveal the subterfuge.

For such a complicated ruse, things go along smoothly—the "agency" murdering anyone who becomes suspicious—until reentry, when the heat shield on the actual spaceship becomes detached. The craft is consumed in the atmosphere, and there is no capsule to restore the men to. The plane carrying them to the rendezvous returns to the air base, where Brubaker and the others quickly piece together what must have happened and realize that they are officially "dead"; hence, their only hope is to escape to a populated area and show themselves.

Stealing the plane they attempt to fly to safety, but there is not enough fuel and they must ditch in the desert. Knowing

NASA will try to kill them before they reveal the plot, they select the three remaining directions and set off singly, hoping one will survive and reach civilization. The hostile environment in which they now struggle for their lives curiously resembles the Mars they never reached. The long-awaited test of endurance on an alien world takes place on Earth. Eventually, NASA recaptures two of the three, but Brubaker turns into a kind of Indian, burying himself in the sand as the choppers fly overhead, then killing and eating a rattlesnake in a cave. He is able to hide out long enough to be discovered and rescued from his pursuers by a persistent reporter (Eliott Gould) and a right-wing crop-dusting pilot (Telly Savalas). Gould and Brolin arrive at a memorial service for the astronauts just as the President is delivering their eulogy. As the two men approach the gathering, the camera pans to each of the relevant shocked faces (the head of NASA, the wives, the corrupt Senator . . .); then the movie ends with an increasingly slow-motion (becoming a freeze frame) of Gould and Brolin running to the moment of truth.

On one level, this is a simple adventure movie based on high-level corruption and cover-up, set somewhere between Watergate and (prophetically) Contragate—or between the Kennedy assassination and the *Challenger* disaster. However, myths from popular culture operate on many levels to reveal truths from the background of our civilization.

As a member of the astronaut program during the 1960s, Brian O'Leary was being trained for an eventual mission to Mars. Like Brubaker, he had high ideals and believed in outer space as the destiny of mankind; he was willing to make sacrifices to explore the unknown. On the surface the one other thing he and Brubaker share is the fact that neither of them actually made it to Mars. However, on the level of a parable, Brubaker speaks O'Leary's subtext throughout the film.

Although O'Leary is not explicitly blackmailed into a role in a space scam, he does realize that the NASA ideology and, in fact, the whole cabal of science is a cover-up of cosmic truth. The exploration of outer space (which even by itself has played second fiddle to SDI for many years) disguises an institutional refusal to look at our true place in the universe. O'Leary left NASA primarily because of budget cuts in the civilian program (and the increasing emphasis on military projects), but subsequently he discovered that space science itself can be a decoy for true science—that

NASA, for instance, would rather create elaborate subterfuges than acknowledge the possible existence (as shown by their own data-tapes) of artifacts of an extraterrestrial civilization on Mars.

Early in *Capricorn One*, after Brubaker and crew are flown from the launch site to Texas, the head of NASA (played by Hal Holbrook) shows them a rocky, sandy stageset of Mars, complete with a replica module on its landing pad. Here is where they are to pretend to descend onto the Martian surface. Here they will receive the message from the President . . . that they have demonstrated how our species, which is capable of pettiness, is also capable of brilliance . . . while standing in a fabricated environment with artificial spotlights on them, pretending to be on Mars. Yet this is the state of science today. It announces wondrous things to the world at the same time as it shamelessly tries to conceal that its view of reality is unravelling. The cosmos of NASA and the space science community seems an ostentatious display of painted paper maché props. Authorities remind us gratuitously that the human race has accomplished great things. However, these "great things" have toxified and depleted our planet, exiled us from our hearts and spirits, and disenfranchised us from our basic powers of healing. Of course scientists have not specifically done all these things, but they have been at the forefront of the sham, which includes an assertion that the universe is a relatively simple and vacuous explosion in which human beings and their minds have arisen by chance and will be obliterated circumstantially. In the short term, if they have not directly participated in degrading the planet (and who hasn't?), they have fostered its companion lie—that science alone is capable of restoring things, that their cabal is our last best hope.

"Do you really think I like this?" Holbrook (as Calloway) asks Brubaker—the technological and scientific establishment addressing the masses. "Look at what we've done. Look at what we've meant to this country. Look at how much more we can do." This is conventional science's famous apology.

Brubaker responds: "[I suppose] if we go along and lie our asses off, then the whole giant world of truth is protected. [And] if we don't go along with some giant ripoff of yours, then we're ruining the country. [But] if the only way to keep something alive is to become everything I hate, I don't know if it's worth keeping alive."

In this book O'Leary holds up the hollow universe of suns

and planets and expanding galaxies and exposes it for the stageset it is. It is not premeditated fake, but it is a vision of only one dimension of reality, a mirage of the actual space in which we dwell. At heart most scientists know this but are terrified by the consequences of abandoning their reality and facing the true unknown. They prefer the illusion of power over the molecules and mechanics of a universe which is infinite beyond comprehension and ultimately consigns all of us to oblivion. They embrace their dead universe, because, at least on an ego level, they can "control" it by their claims to knowing its laws and their pretence of being able to reconstruct its origins. They will fight to the death to defend it because it also represents their ego-states, their professional identities, their salaries.

From an objective standpoint, they give us a stunningly beautiful cosmos of cells and stars—which represents one dimension of reality; O'Leary attempts to reconcile their version with the less apparent internal dimensions of mind and matter. When Brubaker suggests that maybe things don't have to be this way, Calloway responds, "This thing is out of my hands. You think it's all a couple of loony scientists; it's not. It's bigger. It's gotten too big. There are people out there, forces out there, who have a lot to lose. It's in the hands of grown-ups."

The so-called professionals continue to falsify experience—their own as well as ours—in the name of both truth and the protection of innocent people. The more fervent of them are organized into Skeptic groups, which send out licensed scientists and magicians to debunk the mind-matter crossover and paranormal phenomena in general. These people are not concerned with the potential of the human race. Like the oil cartel and the inside arbitragers, they have too much at stake to see their activities with any perspective. They are addicted to their views of reality.

Brian O'Leary has escaped from the desert of the false Mars and he must interrupt the President's eulogy with stunning news: I am alive. Not only am I alive, but the universe is alive, more alive than either of us ever imagined, and more benign and beautiful than this "enlightened" century can bear. Whether we can listen to him or must turn back to the comforts of our daily fraud may determine the fate of our planet.

—Richard Grossinger

INTRODUCTION

> Great spirits have always encountered violent opposition from mediocre minds.
>
> —Albert Einstein

We are living in extraordinary times. On the one hand, we feel the denials and violent opposition of the "mediocre minds" that inhabit our leading governments, universities, corporations and religions. On the other hand, we can sense in the air an uneasy excitement of coming changes whose implications are so enormous we cannot fathom how we may emerge on the other side. Most of us do not have an inkling of what that other side might look like. Regardless, we are on the threshold of a major renaissance in outer and inner space. This book gives evidence on how this process is accelerating us into a Third Millennium that in no way will resemble the Second.

I will be describing catalytic events that prompted me as a traditional scientist to realize at middle age that there is much, much more than meets the eye. Through little conscious choice of my own at first, I slid into an inner universe of such wonder and magnitude, I am still struggling with my "mediocre mind" to allow the truth to unfold. These events began to occur during the late 1970s.

One decade ago I would have best been described as a politically liberal, idealistic, yet traditional scientist, serving on the physics faculty at Princeton University. I had published over one hundred peer-reviewed technical papers in planetary science and astronautics. Earlier, I had been a physics major at Williams College, obtained a masters in astronomy at Georgetown and a Ph.D. in astronomy at the University of California at Berkeley.

By the time I was a graduate student in the 1960s I was actively publishing papers in planetary science. The title of my master's thesis was "The High-Dispersion Absorption Spectrum of a Simulated Martian Atmosphere of NO_2" and my doctoral thesis was entitled "Mars: Visible and Near-Infrared Studies and the Composition of the Surface." Abundant funds from NASA made planetary research a dynamic activity to pursue. The field grew rapidly as robot probes began to unlock some of the secrets of the Moon, Mars, Venus—and later Mercury, Jupiter, Uranus, and Neptune.

Just after receiving my Ph.D. in 1967 I was fortunate enough to be appointed as a NASA astronaut. I was among a group of eleven scientists who trained for potential spaceflight planned for the years following the Apollo program. Because my graduate research was primarily about Mars, and because NASA was talking about completing manned Mars missions during the 1980s, I played a unique role in the astronaut corps: I was the only planetary scientist in the program and therefore seemed destined to go to Mars. But that didn't happen. Sudden budget cuts in NASA, retrenchment in our national confidence and sense of vision, and the war in Vietnam all intervened, and I left the astronaut program without having taken a flight into space and without any prospects of even a trip into orbit for at least fifteen years.

At astronomer Carl Sagan's invitation, I then took an assistant professor appointment in planetary and space science at Cornell University. There I began to be involved in various NASA teams including the Mariner 10 Venus—Mercury Television Science Team. Having left the astronaut program had not turned out to be the disappointment I might have expected: exploring the solar system became the exciting drawing card for me, vicariously exploring new worlds through the eyes of robots on the threshold of new discovery. Being among the first to glean and interpret the data was an extraordinary experience. For example, I discovered and named the largest feature on Mercury—the 1500 kilometer diameter Caloris Basin. I examined the first lunar samples brought to Earth.

One by one the planets revealed themselves to us: their pockmarked surfaces, swirling atmospheres and varied moons. Mars opened to us its unexpected Grand Canyons, huge volcanoes and dried-up river beds. Ideas kept flowing through me about new ways of looking at the planets and their satellites. I researched how we can determine the chemical composition of surface and atmospheric particles from optical properties, how we can search for ancient circular basins on the Moon and planets from their wobbles and their gravity anomalies, and what kinds of future observations could answer fundamental questions about whether or not we're alone in the universe.

In some ways, the results of these planetary missions were disappointing. We didn't find life. Planetary surfaces were ancient and proved either too hot or too cold. Atmospheres turned out to be too thick or too thin. Specialists in geomorphology and atmospheric physics soon took over specific problems in which my interest had waned. By the 1980s, with the cream of discovery seemingly having been skimmed off the planets, a new orthodoxy in planetary science was created that, for me, would turn a remarkably innovative field into a relative humdrum. Crater counts on Mercury and the satellites of outer planets, climatological models of the atmospheres of Venus and Jupiter, and the detailed geomorphological mapping of Mars were not as exciting as the search for life.

Also during the 1970s I had become interested in national politics. I taught courses in technology assessment at the University of California Law School in Berkeley and at Hampshire College. I testified in the U.S. Senate several times on NASA's priorities and then became employed in 1975 as a special consultant on energy for the House Interior Committee. There, I wrote speeches and coordinated hearings for Representative Morris Udall who was then running for President. This experience exposed me directly to the power politics of Washington and its insulation from the long term real interests of the American people. I saw how the candidate himself had to rely on his advisors for making important statements, and how some of the advisors seemed to be more interested in power than in leading.

Meanwhile, at Princeton University, my friend and colleague Gerard O'Neill was conceptualizing a totally new perspective of exploring outer space. He proposed that we could colonize the extraterrestrial void using the resources available to us on the Moon and asteroids. There, the raw materials for designing and actualizing space communities would come cheaply because they sit at the bottom of shallow gravity wells in contrast to the Earth. I appreciated the idea and accepted his invitation to join the physics faculty at Princeton in 1975.

During this period I once again published a number of scientific papers, this time on using the resources of the asteroids and the moons of Mars for creating and expanding a multitrillion dollar industrial infrastructure in space. I led workshops held at the NASA Ames Research Center and Stanford University. Some of the best NASA, university and contractor engineers and scientists participated. I ended up writing and editing several books on these concepts, which were on the forefront of future space alternatives studied during the 1970s. But somehow, these ideas never even inched toward development. Clearly the American outer space effort had sunk into a secondary status, stunningly confirmed for us in 1986 as we watched with horror the *Challenger* disaster.

All during my creative years, from Berkeley to Cornell to Princeton, I was writing books, giving talks, and teaching courses in our exciting exploration of outer space. I taught formal astronomy at Cornell, Hampshire, San Francisco State and the Universities of Massachusetts and Pennsylvania. I taught Physics for Poets at Princeton. Enrollments kept going up, invitations to teach at prestigious universities kept coming in, and I was turning down many offers to publish. I served as board chairman of two space organizations: the National Space Council of the Aerospace Education Association and the Institute for Security and Cooperation in Outer Space. And yet, as we began to enter the 1980s, all the excitement began to wither. We Americans began to lose direction, leadership, consensus and quality research in outer space exploration. The choice for us as individuals in the field seemed to be, either adapt to an unexciting status quo, do weapons research, or become open to something new outside the existing governmental, university, corporate and foundation structures.

As of one decade ago, I began to sense that only the last alternative would work for me. True, I still felt intellectually comfortable with the likes of Sagan and O'Neill, but their world view was soon to be shattered for me. My inner space began to stir.

Having effectively blocked any awareness of a far greater reality during the first two decades of my scientific career, I quite literally stumbled into the new perspective described in this book. One by one, the sacred cows of reductionism and materialism fell before my unbelieving eyes.

I began having psychic experiences. I started communicating telepathically. I had the experience of moving out of my body and floating over cities. I healed myself with my mind. I had a near-death experience. I recalled possible former lives. I felt the presence of other-dimensional intelligence. I explored the rich, colorful textures of inner space. Time and again, I scientifically verified experiments that showed the influence of emotions over the electrical activity of donated white blood cells housed in a laboratory miles away.

In many ways, I was the ideal subject for these experiments. Until I turned forty, I had known little or nothing about their outcomes, so I had no expectations to prejudice the results. This provided all the "proof" I needed to transcend the limited methods and practices of mainstream science.

This book meshes my experiences with a rapidly growing body of scientific findings that require that we radically change our paradigm. The new physics, biology and psychology all point to the reality of our interconnectedness at levels far more profound than the vast majority of us can acknowledge. The universe works in ways far more mysterious than Newton—and even Einstein, Heisenberg and Hawking—could have expressed. For example, we shall find that reconciliation of the four presently known forces of nature into a unified field theory is not adequate to model our reality—a reality that includes both paranormal events and the everyday presence of consciousness itself. Thus, evidence to support the newer view can no longer be ignored.

I also believe that the "great spirits" whom Einstein referred to reside in all of us. But we need to awaken ourselves first because our "mediocre minds" for the most part hold sway over us. We all have these shortcomings to a lesser or greater degree.

For some of us to claim to be in the new spiritual elite—as if this were a new industry that seeks to corner the market—I believe will backfire. We must be humble about this transformation. My weakness is being impatient toward those who do not want to make the necessary changes, and I am finding that this impatience is holding me back from fuller self-discovery. Some of you may detect this tone from time to time in the book.

Regardless, my main point is that, as soon as you are willing to open your mind and experience to the seemingly incredible, you will be taking the first steps toward your own discovery. These actions reinforce the wisdom of the ages: We humans are fundamentally immortal, beyond form, and part of a greater whole that is also embodied in each one of us. I believe that science is at last telling us these things loudly and clearly.

This book has been a challenge to write, in vivid contrast to my previous works, which were more comfortably within the range of our accepted science and technology. Furthermore, I have inexpressible insights that come flooding in, waiting for assimilation into scientifically accurate language. Alas, some of these flashes still remain in the realm of the ineffable. We all have these intuitive breakthroughs, but more often then not they seem to slip away beyond our familiar frames of reference. In many ways, we are dealing with a crisis in our language rather than in the true experience of our reality.

As we shall see in this book, our perspectives about our inner and outer space are profoundly changing. The old models do not seem to work any longer. The lines between the old and the new are being drawn for us to see clearly and many of us are witness to an extraordinary set of experiences for which we don't yet have models.

All rules of science are open to question and we will have an unprecedented opportunity to participate in the grand adventure. The recent achievement of what many are heralding as "cold" table top fusion is symbolic of the likelihood that the science of the future will no longer be the exclusive province of Big Government. As this and many more events continue to unfold during the 1990s, I believe each of us will be able to pierce the veil of denial and enter into a New Millennium of enlightened discovery—of ourselves and of our universe.

I believe we shall find that our changing perception of our outer space is merely a manifestation of the awakening of our inner space. Our own minds have great power in determining our reality. I came to realize that the current practices of Western science and technology were approaching an ultimate boundary of diminishing returns, and that a new, much broader, paradigm was needed. There simply are too many anomalies for our current science to embrace. My experience and that of many others bear out this truth for me, as I hope it will for you as you read this book.

I recently had a dream symbolic of my ambivalence regarding the relationship between mainstream science and my emerging awareness of a greater reality. I was on a village common with some fellow open-minded scientists busily assembling photographs of the "face" on Mars—a feature whose origin remains a mystery, as we shall see in Chapter 5. We worked on card tables and were dressed in ordinary street clothes reminiscent of the commoners of centuries ago, or perhaps of the scientists of the early Renaissance.

Surrounding the common were three gigantic Tudor mansions inhabited by three leading mainstream space scientists (high priests?) well known to me. The mood was familiar and haunting, almost as though we were in more than three dimensions. One of them was standing on his front porch peering out toward me curiously but unconvinced about the professionalism of the activity on the common. (As we shall see, most space scientists claim there is nothing significant about the face on Mars and they ridicule those who attempt to research the existing pictures.) This mainstream scientist and I had eye contact, but we both felt separated from each other. I felt a great distance between them and me. I also felt their disdain; that these powerful men refused to acknowledge, fund or participate in the new work. Our leaders seemed to be totally unaware of the implications of our research.

Those of us on the common were experiencing a lot of excited anticipation about what we were doing, and yet I felt sadly split from the ruling class. I was also envious of their position and power. Our resources were scarce and we could use at least a little financial support—and another mission to Mars. My remorse of separation from former colleagues who had really "made it" in scientific and governmental circles penetrated so deeply within me, that a part of me wanted to walk up to one of the houses, ring the doorbell, and begin to talk to them about our new agenda—if they were willing to meet with me. I still want to do that in waking life, but I know I shall find it difficult.

I have often reflected on this dream. The implications of an ancient civilization on Mars seem to be too unbelievable for my mainstream colleagues to embrace. From my perspective, the new data are valid, begging for answers. Yet I am afraid of being alone, of being ridiculed, of being excommunicated, of being unfraternal.

I also find myself occasionally judging their lack of openness, yet I don't want to demean them. I do not want to create a "them" and "us." I do, however, want to challenge them to explore some of the most exciting frontiers ever faced in the history of science. My brother-in-law, Stuart Heywood, himself an accomplished molecular biologist, once referred to many of his peers as "me too scientists." These are the individuals who seek secure careers, and therefore select projects that mimic earlier work, with minor modifications, in order to obtain the approval and funding from fellow scientists.

We all know that change is never easy, even if it is for the better. We are creatures of habit. And so it will take some time for the explosive realities explored in this book to take hold, perhaps as much as a generation or two. We must be able to tolerate our differences during the transitional process.

This book is an attempt to reach all scientists and interested lay people who seek to understand the extraordinary changes we are experiencing. It is also an invitation to participate in the unfolding adventure.

No problem can be solved from the same
consciousness that created it.

—Albert Einstein

1

THE QUEST FOR REALITY

> The mystical theme of the space age is this: the world, as we know it, is coming to an end. The world as the center of the universe, the world divided from the heavens, the world bound by horizons in which love is reserved for members of the in group: that is the world that is passing away. Apocalypse does not point to a fiery Armageddon but to the fact that our ignorance and our complacency are coming to an end.
>
> —Joseph Campbell

On a recent winter night, John and Lisa were making love in their San Diego hotel room. About five miles away in a downtown laboratory, a strip chart recorder was registering wild fluctuations that measured changes in the electrical activity of a solution of some of Lisa's white blood cells from saliva which she had donated a few hours earlier.

The moment the lovemaking stopped, fluctuations in the electrical current ceased. After a few hours' sleep (and a quiet chart), the activity abruptly started up when a morning lovemaking session began. And just as sharply they both died down together several minutes later.

This scenario may sound like science fiction, but it really happened. Only the names of the participants were changed to protect their anonymity. When I looked at the data, I became convinced beyond any reasonable doubt that the lovemaking and the blood cells were somehow connected. No hoax was involved, and the time correlations were striking. Distance did not seem to matter. This one experiment proved to me as a skeptical scientist that we could measure force fields of communication in consciousness that defy the known laws of physics. Within the context of widely reported and scientifically verified stories involving psychic phenomena, this event was not all that remarkable. But for me it was: I had the data I needed to turn around the denial I had so repeatedly expressed toward the obvious—that the paranormal is the normal and that we humans have somehow created for ourselves a very confining reality. The experiment also showed me that the work of polygraph scientist Cleve Backster needs to be taken seriously. It was the laboratory proof I needed to establish the reality of experiences that transcend mainstream science.

The exciting result was not new. In 1966, Backster had made a discovery that was to change his life and possibly our understanding of how biological systems work. Intrepid experimenter that he was, he decided to hook a leaf of one of his plants up to a lie detector to see if there was any discernible response to watering. Much to his surprise, the plant appeared to respond to his *thoughts* of watering it. The plant behaved just like a person subjected to a lie detector test would react when he experiences a strong mental image or emotion.

In the ten minutes that followed, Backster performed a second experiment that stunned him. He decided to threaten the plant's well being by burning the leaf to which the electrodes were attached. The moment he visualized this, and before he could reach for a match, the chart made a strong move upward. When he returned to the room after finding the matches, and with the matches in hand, he walked toward the plant. There was abrupt change in the chart. When he actually burned the leaf, the reaction of the lie detector was only slight. Attempts to fake a threat to the other leaves that were hooked up met with little response. Evidently, the plants could read his mind and his true intentions.

Many experiments performed over the past twenty years have confirmed Backster's astounding results. These are described in Peter Tompkins' and Christopher Bird's classic book *The Secret Life of Plants*. In spite of all the evidence, many mainstream scientists still do not believe the data, in part because human thoughts and emotions are difficult to quantify, in part because they imply the incredible.

Several later experiments did help to clarify the issues Backster had raised. In one case, Backster poised a basket of brine shrimp to be loaded into a pot of boiling water. A timing mechanism with an arbitrary dumping time was hooked up while Backster, his staff and onlookers left the laboratory. Upon returning he discovered that the plants responded strongly at the time that the brine shrimp met their deaths. His plants seemed to express compassion for fellow living beings. This repeatable experiment virtually eliminated the possible influence of other effects, such as the presence of humans and their thoughts and emotions.

A nearly endless succession of experimental surprises followed. On another occasion, Backster noticed his plants responded to the cracking of a raw egg. He then hooked up the egg to the lie-detector and found electrical activity corresponding to the characteristic heart beat rate of a chick embryo. But the egg was unfertilized! As Tompkins and Bird explain, "He appeared to have tapped into some sort of force field not conventionally understood within the present body of scientific knowledge."

A similar force was actually detected by Yale biologist Harold Saxon Burr fifty years ago. He noticed mysterious patterns of electrical activity associated with multi-cellular organisms. With his collaborator, F.S.C. Northrup, he published results of experiments in which he detected minute electrical patterns in virtually all living matter. He called these electrodynamic fields life fields or L-fields.

However, before I came so quickly to the conclusion that we telepathically communicate our consciousness, I needed to measure all of this for myself. There is no substitute for direct experiments in the laboratory. I had two visits in my San Diego itinerary last summer: one to a friend who is an eminent microbiologist and leader of a prominent skeptics group. The second visit was to Backster. I thought, what a great opportunity this would be to get two people together, both life scientists well trained in laboratory procedures and enthusiastically curious about the mysterious workings of nature.

I showed my biologist friend one of Backster's papers. After a brief reading he handed it back to me saying that, in due respect, he didn't have time to look into these kinds of "far-out" things and that Backster's experiments were not scientifically controlled. He would need either a strong working hypothesis involving a solid scientific principle or some experimental results that would use a second lie-detector system that could serve as a control or zero-reference. The experiment would also need to be repeatable, with the experimental and control devices switched arbitrarily throughout the experiments.

My friend was right, I thought. I was excited about the possibility that Backster was on to something. The true correlation between stimulus and response was excellent, but the controls were not tight. And who was to measure what a thought or an emotion was? And why hadn't universities throughout the world repeated the experiment? When I realized Backster's work was outside the framework of scientific verification in the foreseeable future, I became disappointed, but decided that there was no alternative but to plunge myself into an experiment in which I would be a subject.

Backster was more than cooperative. Assisted one evening by Steve White, a graduate student in marine biology, I donated my white blood cells. This experiment was a repetition of one Backster and White had already carried out with many diverse people. The working hypothesis was that when the electrodes are attached to the donated white blood cells, the electrical resistance in the cells respond to the surges in the donator's emotions. They had published a paper showing strong time correlations between experiencing the emotion (usually negative), as observed or logged by the subject, and the strip chart recording deflection.

In spite of these apparently positive results, there was no substitute for the experience itself. And so, with the lie detector attached to my cells but not to me, I settled into a seat several feet away and was interviewed by both Backster and an old friend who had some personal remarks that at times were to make me feel quite uncomfortable. I was taped on a split screen video, one half on me and one half on the strip chart recorder. The results were striking: as I saw the video replay and I returned to the occasionally uncomfortable feeling I had had while the interview unfolded, I did indeed see strong correlations between the deflections on the strip chart and my uncomfortableness. I couldn't fake it either: attempts to feign a negative emotion met with no response. The correlations had to be real, imposed either as bad news from the outside, or as a spontaneous thought or emotion that came on me before I had a chance to process it mentally.

I left the laboratory to go to the San Diego airport and fly 350 miles back home to Phoenix. The experiment would go for eight hours, after which the donated cells would begin to die. I synchronized my watch with laboratory time and noted events that caused me anxiety: missing the turn onto the freeway, returning the rental car onto a crowded lot, standing in a long line for my plane ticket, nearly missing the flight (it was the last flight out that night), takeoff, landing, discovering my son wasn't there to pick me up at the Phoenix airport, going to the bathroom, going home, and going to sleep.

Backster and I compared notes. We found strong deflections at the times of nearly all of my perceived anxieties with a few deflections in addition. My chart became very quiet after I went to sleep. The results impressed me enormously. If they were valid, we would need to accept the hypothesis that white blood cell donors communicate their emotions to their cells with no apparent attenuation at distances of up to hundreds of miles. The implications were mind-boggling. Evidently, we communicate some fundamental aspect of our consciousness to other living things with which we are somehow connected and the signal does not fall off with large distances.

This experiment suggested an even bolder possibility; when we send astronauts to Mars, what if we hook up their cryogenically stored white blood cells and/or their own house plants remaining on Earth? Then we could measure the stimuli-responses as the astronauts move to vast distances of several light minutes from the Earth. Would their energies still not be attenuated? Would the communication travel at the speed of light, instantaneously, or at some other velocity? The experiments on Earth suggest there is no reduction in signal, unlike what one might expect for electromagnetic waves familiar to the physicist. One would have expected an attenuation proportional to the inverse square of the distance, but that was clearly not the result.

Wanting more confirmation of these bizarre results, I was eager for a second experiment which Backster generously allowed. This time a friend was subjected to the test. Again, the split screen video revealed striking correlations between emotional reactions and recorder deflections. When we returned to our hotel several miles away, I logged events potentially traumatic to my friend, such as turning left on a red light, slamming the hotel door, and bringing up painful issues. The time correlations were uncanny. The recording was again quiet during sleep.

But the most convincing results of all came from the anonymous but reliable source concerning the lovemaking. With a time precision of seconds and with repeated bouts of intensity lasting several minutes over a span of several hours, lovemaking activity was correlated with the wildest sawtooth recordings I have ever seen, miles away in Backster's laboratory. Such a profile did not occur during any other activity and was relatively quiet during other times. A careful examination of the source's chart and time log convinced me that Backster's hypothesis had been proven.

This experiment was the paradigm-shattering culmination of years of my struggling with two very different models of the universe. In the first of them, science was predictably safe. This was the science I had learned in school and taught at universities for most of my career. The second was experiential, unexplainable, and totally outside my familiar ground. I had suspected that the first model was not adequate for the science we really need to be practicing. Now I was finally convinced that reality was truly far vaster and more mysterious than our accepted science can embrace.

The Beginnings of My Struggle

My quest among models of reality began on a spring Sunday in 1977, when I was lying down with 300 others in a dimly lit hotel ballroom on a carpeted floor in a northern suburb of Philadelphia. The instructors were playing soothing music as we sank into a deep dreamlike relaxation, with our eyes closed. Their voices suggested we enter in our minds a perfect setting where we could visualize ourselves having and achieving anything we wanted.

I had never done anything like this before. For the first time since I was a child I felt a purity, a carefreeness, a natural high.

I was in the fifth and last day of a Lifespring training, a human potential workshop which, like EST and a host of others, was designed for us to experience our negative emotions during the first days, and then, having faced them and set them aside, to feel and express the joy of our true selves. On this last day I was definitely in my joy.

My professional colleagues this Sunday would be back in

Princeton fishing, gliding, gardening, taking the family to a fair, grading exams or puttering in the laboratory with their dedicated graduate students. What more inappropriate activity could a physics faculty member at Princeton University be doing, I thought, as I went into my euphoric trance.

What I was undergoing was an unexpected five-day leave of absence from an academic reality to which I would never fully return. Little did I know that then. Little did I know I would be entering a painful decade of decompression from the priesthood of Western, reductionistic science. My change would involve fear, anger, grief . . . and then a profound sense of inner peace, a knowing that their reality had limiting boundaries, a tiny patch in the quilt-work of a far greater reality.

It wasn't that they were wrong. My Princeton physicist colleagues included some of the most brilliant minds on Earth and their contributions to the fabric of reality were substantial. Nobel Laureates and members of the National Academy of Sciences made up a disproportionately high percentage of the prestigious Princeton physics faculty. And down the street were the physicists at the Institute for Advanced Study, where Albert Einstein spent his later years.

While I lay on the floor, I remembered, with detached fondness, the Joseph Henry luncheons at Princeton. Henry had been an eminent nineteenth-century physicist who had made many fundamental discoveries in electricity and magnetism. It was a privilege to sip sherry with the likes of John Wheeler and Eugene Wigner (both Nobel Laureates with profound views on matter, energy and quantum theory), and with Gerard O'Neill and Robert Dicke. Being among forty of the world's top physicists gave me a sense of feeling important, of being at the pinnacle of twentieth-century scientific reality.

Still I also had a vaguely uneasy feeling while hob-nobbing with some of these gentlemen (and they were all men when I was there). I thought perhaps I wouldn't meet their standards, that I might not have quite what it takes to solve the appropriate partial differential equations to make a point. Also, I felt uneasy when some of them quickly dismissed with condescending chuckles others' claims to the paranormal. Debunking was easy for these geniuses.

But something didn't add up. How could millions of claims

of unusual phenomena all be so easily dismissed by judges sitting in the controlled comfort of Jadwin Hall? Even if the overwhelming majority of these claims were misrepresentations or exaggerations, did my colleagues know so much about the nature of the universe, of mind and matter, that they could afford to ignore the whole territory of the as-yet unexplained? Was not their closed-mindedness forcing a negative answer that preempted inquiry among the scientific establishment? Was this a matter of self-protection, or a fear of the unknown? Or was there just too much "real science" to be done to take the time to address what was (to them) almost surely only a hoax or wishful superstitious thinking?

On that beautiful spring Sunday in May, lying there in an altered state of consciousness, my life was beginning to change profoundly. I was to get my own answer to the question of whether or not there was a reality beyond my university knowledge. I was to experience a deep intuition—as real as an image of the Earth in space—an intuition that psychic experiences are real and, therefore, that many related phenomena such as UFO contacts and universal consciousness might be real too. The box I was about to open may have been Pandora's to those who feared to look; but for me it became a wonderful opportunity to explore new realms of experience.

My First Paranormal Experience

I was now sitting up on the ballroom floor cross-legged looking into the eyes of a randomly selected partner, an unremarkable looking woman from Allentown, Pennsylvania, in her late thirties, about my age.

Continuing my euphoric concentration, I then lay back down on the floor and the woman gave me the name of a man, his age, and where he lived (Allentown). I was asked to describe him using psychic powers that I had no conviction were within me. I know nobody from Allentown, which was about a hundred miles from where I was living at the time. My mind doubted that there was any meaning to this exercise. I had not been educated to believe there could be anything real about telepathy. The demonstration of such powers was all idle speculation to me. Nevertheless, I stayed with the exercise, once again going into a deep trance.

An image came up. I saw myself seeing the man, dark haired

and in his forties, walking along a beach on the west coast of Maui in Hawaii. He was without a woman and somewhat sad about it, as he walked into an idyllic make-believe house I had made for him. I showed him globes and maps. He asked questions and we had a strong rapport. We looked up at big billowing clouds, wafting above palm trees which were blowing in the wind. In this imaginative mock-up we shared, he was teaching me about the climate and physical geography of the Hawaiian Islands. I knew I wasn't guessing. I was either "channeling" some truth or imagining something vivid. My female partner then broke into my reverie to inform me that the man had lost his wife by death, was a meteorologist and journalist by profession, and had spent much time on Maui. She said my description fit him to a T.

When the ballroom lights broke our spell, the others began to take a break, but I still lay on the floor in a euphoric state, letting people climb over me. Minutes later I got up. I felt as if gravity had eased. Effortlessly I glided across the room to a glass of water. For the first time I knew how the astronauts must have truly felt when they first arrived in space. I felt like a child again—immersed in a vivid memory of being six and climbing Mt. Monadnock in New Hampshire, with the gigantic rock slabs, white clouds, deep blue sky, the smells and sounds of mossy woods and bubbling streams.

The New Adventure Begins

Thirty years of deadness, I thought. Thirty years of left-brain programming at schools and universities, reciting rote memory to advance myself and to please others. Thirty years of making the true joys of life seem like an escape, a simulation of reality, a day at Disneyland where the replica Matterhorn was the real Matterhorn. I felt I had been brain-damaged, that I had missed out on life.

Who am I? I asked. Where did I come from? Where am I going? What is the real nature of the universe? Not even a Bachelors degree in physics from Williams College, nor a Masters in astronomy from Georgetown, nor a Ph.D. in astronomy from Berkeley (Doctor of *Philosophy* seems a misnomer), nor my astronaut training, nor my faculty positions at Cornell, Caltech, Berkeley, San Francisco State, Hampshire, UMass and Princeton, nor my Congressional staff positions and Presidential candidate advisory positions, nor my books and 100 articles published in prestigious journals, nor my Catholic upbringing—none of this now mattered. For thirty years I had distracted myself from me —the only one who could really find the answers, or begin to find them. These questions, these experiences, transcended the intellectual sphere, a tiny world embedded in a much larger fabric of reality.

My new adventure had begun. I felt like an inner space astronaut eager to share his experience. I began to tell my friends, but many of them reacted with odd looks and forced listening. It then occurred to me that maybe they weren't that interested in inner life, mine or theirs. I couldn't really prove my experience to them, nor could I allow them to share it. In fact, the more enthusiastically I shared my experiences and ideas, the more their impact on my friends seemed to diminish. I was later to realize that these inner events were not a function of the ego-reality. They were to be treasured as something uniquely personal, uniquely me. But they could also be pieced together with experiments into a new reality.

Like many of the astronauts of outer space, my own return to "Earth" was a challenging task. I had experienced something so special and beautiful, it could not be adequately expressed on this level. The afterglow began to fade.

Ultimately, I knew I couldn't tell my scientific colleagues anyway because the experience was subjective and not a controlled experiment. I had thirty years of hard-earned turf to protect and I wasn't about to blow it. So as the days and weeks passed, I returned to normal living and the experience evaporated, to linger only as a memory or curiosity. Meanwhile, it was business as usual at Princeton, hob-nobbing with the physics elite and talking about our research and hobbies and the "real" universe.

In retrospect, that was the only practical thing for me to do. Shirley MacLaine could risk her credibility and be ostracized, but she wasn't among guardians of the old reality at Princeton. I, in contrast, needed to stay underground. I had all to lose and nothing to gain in expressing the benefits of psychic phenomena. I would be debunked, ridiculed, thrown out, and then ignored.

This prognosis didn't stop my quest, however. In the eight years that followed, I continued my "straight" life as a scientist at Princeton and then at Science Applications International Corporation in California, an industrial think tank for the Government.

During the 1980s I was deeply divided between being a corporate scientist and a spiritual seeker. On weekdays I would be at my desk writing proposals or on airplanes flying to NASA Centers and large aerospace companies to pitch our company's capabilities so we could possibly win a contract. On weekends I would be secretly taking courses at the Insight Transformational Seminars, Koh-E-Nor University, and the Prana Theological Seminary. I became an ordained minister at the Movement of Spiritual Inner Awareness, a loosely knit organization whose only real credo is that God is within each of us and that we can gain access to joy through meditation.

As my experiences multiplied and interwove through the years, I became more confident of their lesson. I lived in two widely separated realities, moving back and forth between them, sometimes with excitement and sometimes in pain. I would find myself, for example, driving down the mountain from a spiritual retreat at Lake Arrowhead on a typical weekend, and back into the smog-filled Los Angeles basin to resume work as usual.

My dual life of physics and metaphysics was doomed. In early 1987, I was laid off from my aerospace job primarily because I did not want to work on Reagan's lucrative "Star Wars" Strategic Defense Initiative (SDI) program, where nearly all the new money and action were directed. During the following year, I spent a lot of time publicly opposing SDI. This was yet one more distraction from encountering my expanded reality head-on.

During my twelve years of living in duality, my personal life also had taken many twists and turns. A divorce was followed by painful relationships. I was restless but always seeking. I never gave up, yet I was finding it more difficult by the day to deal with the community of scientists and engineers, on the one hand, and my intuition of a more complex and yet more united mind-matter universe, on the other.

I was also grieving the loss of my colleagues. Carl Sagan, with whom I had taught and researched at Cornell, began to ignore me; he had his own "Cosmos" agenda to sell. A similar parting of the ways even happened with my friend and colleague Gerry O'Neill at Princeton. I was publishing less and perishing more. My exit out the back door of the scientific establishment took ten years and was without fanfare. It might have been less painful to have called a press conference and ceremoniously announced my leaving, but it didn't happen that way.

In fact, it was so gradual that many of my colleagues may not have even noticed that I had walked away and into the forbidden territory. Some did: one took offense when he read the last chapter of my book, *Mars 1999*, in which I fictionally hypothesize telepathic communication between people on Earth and astronauts inhabiting a Mars base in the year 2020. Another used the crude cliche: "Don't open your mind so much that your brains spill out." This person had seen me on television on the Phil Donahue Show: I had appeared on a panel that included not only best-selling author and alleged UFO contactee Whitley Strieber, but also a channel, and actress Joyce DeWitt, whose path is reminiscent of Shirley MacLaine's.

But it has only been during the past year that I have been able to embrace the greater reality. It has required disaffiliating with existing institutions. This time I needed to do it in a loving and forgiving, not an angry, way. It will probably take others less time to let go, since the majority of people have not had the degree of scientific programming I have had. Much of my metaphysical education has been simply my own "uneducation."

In most of the chapters that follow I will be exploring some currently inexplicable phenomena of inner and outer space that are susceptible to scientific inquiry and have also been a crucial part of my own recent experience. The book is a series of snapshots taken of one man's perspective of a rapidly changing world view. It is an astronaut's view of an Earth from which we cannot sufficiently distance ourselves to make it entirely visible no matter how big the rockets we build or how far we may go.

The book may appear naive to those who have mastered the field of metaphysics and practice it in their daily lives. But, having been thoroughly indoctrinated into Western science, I enter these new realms with a special perspective that may help make the transition of others easier. I'm still in between.

Research into unusual phenomena, combined with accelerating numbers of personal experiences, provide an ever-growing body of evidence that we must awaken in order to build a new paradigm of science. There is no turning back. Those scientific and political leaders who choose to ignore this new, emerging paradigm are like the Popes and Cardinals of the Renaissance who objected to the radical ideas of Copernicus, Bruno, and Galileo. Most scientists nowadays are the high priests of an old order striving to defend what is safe for their belief and livelihood. Meanwhile, a larger reality guides some of the rest of us toward a world as large and complex as Newton and Einstein imagined when they went searching for the mind of God.

The New Reality of Inner and Outer Space

What is this greater reality? It basically expands our framework for inquiry. It views the mind as more than a brain compiling information like a mere computer. It views human consciousness as part of a greater reality in (and perhaps beyond) time and space, not as the epiphenomenon of an organism with a limited time span in a physical body. It seeks to integrate the subjective with the objective, the right brain with the left brain. It strives toward the unity of all things rather than the reduction of all things into physical components.

The new reality presumes an interconnectedness, a higher order in the universe that cannot be explained simply by known physical laws. It observes the power of the mind. It weighs hypotheses that dare to challenge existing theories or assumptions. It investigates a variety of approaches to the search for extraterrestrial intelligence, not only the scientifically accepted radio telescopic search, but UFO encounters and the "monuments on Mars". It considers dimensions beyond time and space, concepts beyond matter and energy as currently understood, and realms beyond the physical. It looks beyond Newtonian physics (levers, pulleys, or ramps) to explain how the blocks comprising the Egyptian pyramids, Incan fortresses, Stonehenge pillars, and the Easter Island statues got erected. All of these predated Newton anyway, so have little historically to do with modern mechanics. It regards the possibility that the Earth is one living organism, with its inhabitants behaving like unaware fleas crawling on an elephant.

Our reality is shaped by both our inner and outer perceptions, what I call inner and outer space. Exploring outer space beyond the Earth is the best contemporary example of probing a vast, in fact limitless, frontier, and so is the most appropriate symbol of our quest for knowledge and experience in the depersonalized exterior realm. When I use the expression "outer space," I am referring to *all* our outer experience that is susceptible to language and can be related to others. It comprises most of our daily focus and discourse. We emerge like cell cultures moving outward into an unexplored, often empty void.

Exploring inner space is an entirely different matter. Its frontiers are also vast but they are too subtle for most of us to choose to enter, and they are not vast in either a linear or multidimensional topological way. As an adult, and until about twelve years ago, I was totally unaware of my own inner space awaiting exploration. I believed that everything that could be experienced was "out there," accessible to us outside our bodies in the three dimensions of space and the one dimension of time. For virtually all of us, the outer is the object of our primary conscious focus here on Earth: that is how we get along on this planet at this time; that is how we view survival hunting from amoebas to leopards to tribes of humanoids. By contrast, most of our inner experience has nothing to do with this outer world, and so we have no frame of reference in which to relate the inner to something linear and concrete.

But meanwhile, more and more of us are becoming aware of our expanding inner reality. Much of it cannot be described or mapped. This inner reality may come to us at first as flashes, so elusive that the outer reality quickly takes over and erases any trace of them. But if the inner reality keeps coming back again and again with experiences such as those described in this book, it deserves acknowledgment, especially if the results could include the enhancement or our health and our happiness, the solution to economic, ecological, and energy problems, and an awakening to the realization of our immortality. Yet if we so choose, we can still continue to snuff our inner selves by inordinately filling our lives with activities of the outer. That is all too easy to do in today's externally oriented world, where most of us fail to venture very far into the inner realms.

How is it, then, that we have been ignoring our inner nature and the territories open to it? Why do we seem to be so stuck upon the realities of ordinary space-time and of physical mortality? I suggest that it is *only* because we have chosen to do this. A big "only"! Granted, the pressure to conform to our materialistic, mortal existence is enormous. But I believe we can transcend this. We each can actualize our own reality.

I am proposing that the new reality be defined as comprising at least three major elements. First, it embraces experience with regard to which rational inquiry is still possible, but a fit with existing models may not be possible; therefore, *all* models are open to question. Second, an understanding of the new reality includes outer *and* inner space, as in a cosmic dance between the observer and the observed. Third, it includes the hypothesis that we each shape our own reality: the state or condition of our inner space profoundly influences our experience of what is real in our outer space.

New models will be needed to comprehend this new reality and we do not have many good ones yet. No matter how intelligent or insightful some people may appear, no one person has all the answers to date. The blended territory of inner and outer is so uncharted that we need a generation of "new scientists" who must be both adventurous and cautious about their findings.

The New Scientist

The new scientist, then, is what I would call the sort of person who devises experiments to test phenomena such as telepathic communication between humans and plants and between humans and their donated white blood cells. New scientists would be those who propose theories that explain the strange forms and habits seemingly communicated across time and space within a given species. They would measure unexplained energy anomalies around ancient stone megaliths such as ultrasonic pulses at the time of equinox sunrise. They would endeavor to piece together these phenomena under a broader framework, one that assumes the observer influences the observed and systems change when parts align. They would participate in group consciousness experiences such as human waves in stadiums and transformational workshops. They would employ technology such as dowsing and Kirlian photography to measure changes in the energy fields of human bodies observed during emotional shifts. They would invent a "physics" that transcends electromagnetic, gravitational, and nuclear forces. They would require a biology that goes beyond genetics and molecules.

The seeker of the truth about the new reality is not some gullible oaf believing every scam; he or she also seeks to separate truth from hoax and hyperbole. Many individuals and groups are unscientific in their approach and can distort the truth. The new scientist must be careful to discriminate. One example of an anomalous experience that ended up having a mundane explanation was when I was backpacking with a friend in the Cascades in Washington State about twenty-five years ago. When I lay down to sleep with my ear to the ground and my teeth together, I began to hear a radio station inside my head. We were miles from other people. Whenever I lifted my head to ask my friend whether she heard the station (she said "no"), it stopped. Then it resumed when I lay down again. I distinctly heard the station's name, location on the dial and the fact that it was in Seattle, and I seemed stuck with the loud rock music that I didn't enjoy. What was it? I was later to verify a theory I developed that it was simply my massive silver tooth fillings acting as an antenna to "tune" into that station. This was *not* ESP.

So the new scientist needs to carefully address only those phenomena that are susceptible to scientific inquiry and accessible to personal experience for interested individuals. In this book we shall find several such examples. We do not need to resort to speculative sensationalism or ad-hoc thinking that would impair the credibility of the greater reality. But we shall find that we do not need to throw out the baby with the bath water.

For the new scientist, the new reality is really an old reality. Eastern philosophies and American Indian cultures have embraced its subjective and experiential aspects for centuries. But we're now coming into a time of great opportunity where experiments and experiences may well combine into entirely new syntheses of ancient and contemporary models of reality.

As we begin to awaken, we shall see that the periphery of Western science is now moving rapidly outward from its small place within the fabric of reality. Soon we shall come into a whole new awareness far richer than we ever imagined. In the following chapters you will learn why and how this is happening for those of us who chose to explore the new reality.

Transformation

Transformation is the key concept in this movement into the new reality that I am proposing. While it seems overused at times, the significance of transformation lies in its being more than just change or revolution in the traditional sense. Taken to its roots, transform means "going *beyond* form." We are on the threshold of a great age of transformation some call the Aquarian Age. Every two thousand years, like a wobbling top, the Earth's axis precesses one-twelfth of the way around a complete circle in the sky passing from one sign of the Zodiac into another. Just as Jesus Christ was the focus of the beginning of the Piscean Age, many today believe that the present era is beginning to bring in a new age. Within this context, the new reality is not just a passing fad.

One of the most important books on the personal and social context of transformation is Marilyn Ferguson's *The Aquarian Conspiracy.* Her account was a compilation of developments in virtually every area of transformation. Now, only ten years later, rapid developments in the transformational sciences and global events demand another look at the new age from a down-to-Earth scientific perspective.

Even Freudian psychologists tell us implicitly that the first step in personal transformation is taking responsibility for one's thoughts and actions: In order truly to understand and encompass the new reality and the transformational sciences, we must first transform ourselves. This approach does not work at universities like Princeton. Transformational scientists must not only dispassionately measure phenomena in laboratories. They must allow themselves to become an aspect of the larger phenomena they are attempting to measure. And it is not enough only to read about psychics, the paranormal, reincarnation, healings and UFOs in order to understand the new reality. The *experience* of transformation is center stage for each and every one of us.

My 1977 Lifespring experience was my first significant exposure to personal transformation. In that workshop, and in many I was to take later, participants had the opportunity to confront their fears, their anger, their separation, their guilt, their greed, their jealousy. The result was a transformation of those willing to risk looking at their negative qualities. Awareness of joy and insight followed an initially painful process.

It is truly incredible to observe individuals, who are at first feeling lonely, separate and depressed, come, one by one, out of their closets and become the radiant joyful beings they potentially are. It is also exciting to participate in a feeling of group joy, of oneness: The group also transforms. The problem is, when the seminar ends, the group disbands and individuals soon return to "real" life. The intense experience becomes superficial as it becomes only a memory.

Through practice, practice, practice, individuals can transform, and groups can transform. This I intuit from personal experience. And, with practice, I believe that nations can transform and the world can transform. But unfortunately we need to keep looking at and feeling new painful things about ourselves—the dark night of the soul, the illusion of separation—before the transformation can take place. The traditional spiritual teachers have confirmed this "through shadow into light" process. Before the transformation can take place each of us must be willing to let go of things dear to him or her. Transformation is not very pleasant at first. Acts of great loving come axiomatically only after encountering pain.

My transformation is more a process than a realization, as the next chapter will show. I still need to transform my perception of a hostile world making unwise choices and not going my way. But I do believe that there is a congruence between individual and planetary transformation. On the other side of the transformation lies enlightenment and expansion—yours, mine and the world's.

Planet Earth is also going through its dark night of the soul and is poised to transform. We are forced to look not only at our own individual realities but also at planetary realities. The glue that is holding us together—the economics, politics, environment, and religions—is faltering. The late Buckminster Fuller gave our spaceship Earth only a few years to survive unless we mend our ways.

It sometimes seems that nothing short of the "miracle" of transformation will have the power to heal in time. As Joseph Campbell put it in the quote at the beginning of this chapter, despite ourselves our ignorance and our complacency are coming to an end. We will soon discover that the condition of the world *is* a personal matter.

I believe that our awareness of and participation in the planetary transformation process is about ten to twenty years behind the personal transformation process. In the 1950s and 1960s a small collection of humanistic psychologists began to experiment with individual transformation, which has now blossomed into a large industry. In 1968 a planetary consciousness arose from the first striking pictures of the whole Earth taken by astronauts voyaging to the Moon, and with it the subsequent environmental movement is just now beginning to have a significant influence on our awareness.

This book is a transforming scientist's perspective on his own change and that of society at large. I suspect many of you are now anticipating, undergoing, struggling with, or completing within yourselves, aspects of this change. Having undergone much of this change already individually, I know some of you who will be seeking, as I am now, a sense of social responsibility, of wanting to help others. I ask myself, could it be that my struggles are everybody's struggles, that my alienation is everybody's alienation from a too-slowly changing world embedded in an endlessly changing universe?

The transformational process is about creating a new unity, something that never existed before, something whose new form was not planned, anticipated or hypothesized by most of us. The discoveries need not all come about within the province of a scientific elite. Despite their impressive credentials, an army of astronomers and geologists do not "own" the massive and unique planets of the solar system, and biologists and psychologists do not regulate the relationship between mind and matter. The ability to discover, to make quantum leaps, to transform, is, I believe, within each of us.

In the following chapters, I will describe pathways that I took either by my free will or because they were imposed on me. They have led me, serendipidously, to many new awarenesses that I believe you too can experience. I outline experiments you can perform to reveal some mysteries of the greater reality. Many of these a scientist can repeat in the laboratory, if he must, to "prove" we can all become unstuck and flow into this exciting, joyful future. Any *one* such discovery acknowledged by the scientific community might change the world. For those of you who are scientists, especially skeptics, I ask you to suspend judgement and to allow yourself to be open to an unknown experience.

The next chapter describes my own transformational process with respect to our civilization. It addresses that part of me which is socially conscious but initially fearful and angry. I am poised on the threshold of what feels to me to be a transformation toward love for everything and everybody. But, I haven't reached the goal of this transformation yet; most of us haven't, however socially conscious we may be at present.

Bibliography

Backster, Cleve, "Evidence of a Primary Perception in Plant Life," *International Journal of Parapsychology*, Vol. 10, p. 329 (1968).

Backster, Cleve and Stephen G. White, "Biocommunications Capability: Human Donors and *In Vitro* Leukocytes," *International Journal of Biosocial Research*, Vol. 7, p. 132 (1985).

Campbell, Joseph, interviewed by Eugene Kennedy, "Earthrise: The Dawning of a New Spiritual Awareness," *The New York Times Magazine*, April 15, 1979, pp 14-15.

Tompkins, Peter and Christopher Bird, *The Secret Life of Plants*, Harper and Row, New York (1973).

2

THE WORLD OF ILLUSION AND A RAY OF HOPE

> Let us suppose that two men who regard each other as enemies are in the same lifeboat. Each feels insecure about the designs of the other. Each possesses a drill. Now let us further suppose that each man feels the best way of protecting himself against the other is to threaten to drill a bigger hole in his end of the boat than the other is capable of drilling at his end. The psychotic nature of such an episode is readily apparent, yet this is the essential nature of the nuclear dilemma in the modern world . . . the central meaning of the atomic age is there is no defense except peace.
>
> —Norman Cousins, *The Pathology of Power*

Tired of the petty bickering and lack of issues in recent electoral campaigns? Tired of the impersonality of bureaucracies and medical facilities? Tired of reaping the unwanted side effects of prescribed and unprescribed drugs? Tired of pursuing out-of-date values and goals at the work place? Tired of the unpredictability of the economy and the budget and trade deficits? Tired of an overbloated defense budget? Tired of seeing our planet's rivers and forests and air and life-forms deteriorate? Tired of U.S. Government coverups? Tired of lawyers? Tired of divorces? Tired of religions that preach only dogma and create guilt and fear? Tired of shallow leadership without vision or goals? Tired of the news depicting violence and selected world dramas without a coherence of purpose?

If so, we *do* have alternatives. We *can* transform ourselves and our institutions. From our inner selves we can create a better world and go out and live it. We can aspire to an entirely new social agenda of human affairs which is already practiced by some individuals and groups and spreading worldwide. The new Soviet Union is no accident. Yet even those in lifelong government service have only the flimsiest explanations for what seems a miracle of spontaneous cure. The concept of a transformed society is denied by most of us because we are fearful that by the process of transformation we may lose our jobs, our money, our possessions, our social standing, and our credibility. But many of us have made the leap and survived.

The new reality that I have suggested has its own agenda, one that is bold and more revolutionary than any events that have swept us with the tides of history in an already tumultuous century. As we are about to close the millennium, we are reaching beyond the information age, beyond the computer age, beyond the atomic age, beyond the space age, into a "cosmic intelligence" age. This new age is no longer a small collection of crystal-cleaners, 1960s dropouts, psychics, channels, UFO-logists, parapsychologists and transpersonal psychologists. The greater reality, while unacknowledged publicly and unfunded by political and industrial leaders, also includes George Bush's mainstream America, corporate America, the Pentagon, the university labs, our homes, schools, and churches, for there is only one universe, and as the old sages remarked, those who are willing, the Fates lead; the unwilling they drag along. The greater reality isn't some Whole Life Expo or countercultural fair that the defense establishment can just blow off the Earth. It is bigger than Trident missiles or SDI lasers. It has the teeth of the Lion of Narnia and the wingspread of Don Juan Matus' Eagle. It is the ultimate weapon.

Based on my extensive experience with American public policy as an insider, I believe we are in a period of stagnation which will eventually lead to economic and ecological chaos and will therefore have to yield to the larger global agenda. What will replace it will be totally different, so different it is hard to imagine. But we can make some guesses and we can set goals that allow us to move into the personal and global transformation that I earlier described.

We may be embarking on the greatest revolution of human history. We are talking about more than encountering extraterrestrial intelligence, obtaining scientific proof of survival of physical death and of reincarnation, of non-ordinary consciousness communication, miraculous healing, and multi-dimensional travel. When the veil of illusion is lifted, each of us will come into a much expanded awareness of who we are and of our own immortality, not as religious doctrine but as a living reality.

As individuals, we can make a conscious choice to embrace the new reality now. We don't have to wait until the whole world, as consensus reality, adopts it. We may begin to develop a political and social context that we and others will be unable to ignore.

From Swords to Plowshares: From Star Wars to Mars

There is no better example of the older reality in full operation than that of the current policies and pronouncements of the U. S. Government concerning defense and space. The most striking instance of a Reagan-era fading influence is the potentially massive Strategic Defense Initiative (SDI), or "Star Wars" space weapons program. I have had opportunities to assess this program from the perspective of a contracting industrial scientist and as Chairman of the Board of Directors of the Washington-based think tank, the Institute for Security and Cooperation in Outer Space. We have found much more appealing options for the American people than the SDI, much better modes of security.

One alternative is for the United States to make a commitment with the Soviets to send humans to Mars near the turn of the century. This would be the centerpiece of a world-wide renaissance in space and on Earth. The United States could demilitarize its foreign policy, significantly reduce its nuclear weapons, scrap research and development on space weapons programs, and balance the federal budget and trade deficit.

As you can see, the pay-off of exploiting these opportunities is staggering. Soviet space leaders have repeatedly invited Americans to join them in replacing weapons with the joint trip to Mars. Academician Roald Sagdeev, former head of the U.S.S.R. Space Research Institute and space advisor to General Secretary Gorbachev, has proposed that the joint mission take place in the year 2001. He recently told me that Mr. Gorbachev is ready to set the goal jointly with the U.S. President as soon as we both reconvert our manpower and money from the space weapons programs.

The Mars program would cost the U.S. less than the $3.7

billion per year currently spent on SDI research and development, and a tiny fraction of the full Star Wars were it deployed. Going to Mars would have far greater benefit politically, scientifically, economically and, yes, for national security and world security. A large number of scientists and policy analysts join me in concluding that Star Wars cannot possibly provide its originally promised leakproof screen against a Soviet nuclear attack. Moreover, it could spiral the arms race into a new multi-trillion dollar phase.

History has shown that research on weapons programs, when it surpasses the billion-dollar per year mark, is hard to stop. Two billion one dollar bills laid end-to-end would extend from the Earth to the Moon. We have created a powerful vested interest. Yet even the most vocal SDI critics advocate spending one to three billion dollars per year for research and development on space weapons. But SDI is simply part of the old reality.

Through negotiation and verification, space weapons research and development in both the U.S. and U.S.S.R. can still stop, and we both can find ways to reallocate those resources to the Mars mission, the commercial development of space, increased global security and a higher quality of life. New research projects could include arms control verification, environmental protection, safe energy, efficient transportation, improved health care, the relief of world hunger, and not least of all, the onset of the technologies of the new sciences such as levitation, UFO research, consciousness research, and healing.

The Republican commitments to SDI appear to be iron-clad, but Mr. Gorbachev is ready to talk about a radical change in world view. In 1961, just four months after his inauguration, President John F. Kennedy set the goal of landing a man on the Moon before the end of the decade. George Bush could do this for Mars by the millennium.

My research for *Mars 1999* has shown that this is an excellent year to go there jointly with the Soviets. We have the technology to complete the Mars mission by 1999. We could send two spacecraft (one U.S., one Soviet) with small international crews. Each would be the emergency backup for the other and frequent crew exchanges could take place as in the 1975 Apollo-Soyuz astronaut-cosmonaut exchange. Could you imagine the public impact of the two superpowers sending, respectively, an astronaut and a cosmonaut to the surface of Mars in the name of all humankind?

Aside from the obvious political benefits, we will have the opportunity to search for life on the most Earth-like of planets. Chapter 5 discusses some remarkable features on Mars that we could investigate firsthand during the 1999 mission: possible monuments erected by an intelligent civilization. We can begin to process materials from the tiny Martian moons that will provide fuel for later visits, leading to a Mars base, lunar base, and space settlements.

We need a specific goal like this to rekindle the public imagination and as a symbol of our new-found but untested friendship with the Soviets. We need to awaken NASA from its twenty-year coma.

But we must move quickly. As cosmonaut Georgii Grechko recently said, "We must go together to Mars. Otherwise we'll go there ourselves."

I can recall being an eight year old boy at an open house at Harvard College Observatory; it was the night Truman upset Dewey in the 1948 election. I looked through the telescope at Saturn and Mars with a sense of wonder. These fuzzy glows were whole worlds, different from this one in every way. What did an election of mere Earthmen matter? From that time, even though there was no space program, my nearly single-minded purpose has been to explore space.

I voraciously read magazines containing the visions of Wernher von Braun and other space pioneers. The crossroads at which we now stand were already forming in the futuristic science and science fiction of the 1940s and early 1950s: On one hand, we could send people and robots to the Moon, planets and stars to enhance our knowledge, search for other life, and even colonize other worlds; or, on the other hand, we could live and die in the shadow of nuclear weapons and space weapons.

I remember the strange sensation that part of me fantasized about international trips to Mars, and about the search for extraterrestrial life. While part of me lived under the shadow of fallout shelters, Stalin, McCarthy, Hiroshima, and the decline of the United States from a compassionate world leader to an impersonal collaborator with military might and business profit on an unprecedented scale. President Eisenhower prophesied his own legacy when he warned of the power of the military-industrial complex.

As an adult, I was to play several roles in pointing out how the Government could redirect its scientific and technological priorities toward peaceful projects. The roles included astronaut, university scientist, Congressional staff member, industrial scientist, and public policy think tank leader. In them, I saw the repetitive themes pervade major decisions about the public funding of science and engineering in the United States: by playing on the fears of the American people, big money could be made continuing to manufacture weapons.

To my dismay, I discovered that the revolving door between government and industry provides enormous, legal cash rewards for the policy-makers at the top. And this is quite aside from the famous $5,000 screwdrivers procured by the Pentagon. It is no wonder that Star Wars has become so popular. As the largest research and development effort ever funded by the Government, it has become the Pentagon's new trillion-dollar toy. Details of legal and illegal self-serving activities near the top (in the name of national security) are well documented in Norman Cousins' *The Pathology of Power.* Meanwhile, most of us seem to have lost the perspective that the United States and Soviet Union are each perpetrating a myth that the other nation is a potential enemy to be defended against to the hilt.

That we Americans have become so mesmerized in defensive fear typifies a world view that hopefully may be only temporary. At present, we appear to have little real choice in elections; the media usually foresees only warfare, chaos, destruction and scandal over peace and love; the various lobby and special interest groups appear to have lost the true meaning of human compassion; our civilian space program has been without a purpose since the Apollo days and has virtually ground to a halt while Reagan and Bush played Star Wars. Our political leaders have lost the courage of their convictions; they have lost their sense of positive vision for our children, and lost our place in history as a nation born of ideals. These are some of the issues that confront the United States and in fact confront an entire world poised on the brink of destruction.

The fear is insidious. It is covered by a slickness and sense of temporary comfort as we grasp for an ever higher standard of material living. Opportunities are provided for a select few to make quick profit by manipulating the monetary system. But these schemes are bound to collapse, as "Black Monday" 1987 has shown. That we have not learned our lesson and continue to feast in the shadow of our denial is shown by the quick rebound of the international money game. The stock market crash is but a warning shot across the bow that foreshadows how the old game, the older reality, will not work in the long run.

I do not mean to absolve the Soviet Union from the world terror game. They have been every bit as aggressive as the Americans. They play fear games just as well. Moreover, their government has until at least very recently severely limited human freedom through open repression and torture.

Those of us whose senses feel dulled by all the bad news I have chronicled thus far may have difficulty understanding or believing the good news. But just as surely as we are deluged by Iran-Contra scandals, weapons profiteering and the billions spent on Star Wars, we are also reviving von Braun's drama of international human trips to Mars, and Buckminster Fuller's vision of converting weaponry to "livingry." More than any single event in this century of unprecedented terror, the rise of Mikhail Gorbachev to power in the Soviet Union seems to open the world to the possibility of a positive future.

It has been Gorbachev (not Reagan or Bush) who has made the major concessions in arms limitations talks. It is Gorbachev who has declared no first strike and wants a nuclear free world by the year 2000. It is Gorbachev who wants to negotiate a halt to Star Wars. It is Gorbachev who wants to go to Mars together in the year 2000. It is Gorbachev who has encouraged a new freedom of expression and debate among the Soviet people. It is Gorbachev who led the withdrawal of Soviet troops from Afghanistan.

Is this all deception? I doubt it, although the results remain to be determined. Following recent visits to the Soviet Union, I became convinced that *glasnost* (openness) is real. Even if it is deception, it may be too late to reverse. The peace genie is out of the bottle; it is part of the new reality; and I do not believe that any amount of repression, terror, propaganda, or even change in leadership can stuff it back in.

We will have bad moments. We may even fail; but there is presently an opening in the miasma of cold war. The news from the Soviet Union is indeed good news, and even if we are wary of its reality, the reality will prevail nevertheless. Arms control verification is an obvious interim solution as trust builds up.

The pressing question then is this: how can we convert our trillion dollar profit-making and federally bankrupting war machine to peaceful projects that will allow us to clean up the planet and move to higher levels of consciousness on Earth and in space? In the final analysis, how can we convert our collective fear to love?

Personal and Professional Changes

Even though I hadn't yet begun to grasp the importance of the transformative sciences, some of my most positive experiences occurred during the 1960s. These were the Apollo years, John F. Kennedy's dramatic setting of the lunar landing goal and its fulfillment in 1969. During that time, I received a Ph. D. from Berkeley in astronomy, was appointed a professor of space sciences at Cornell University, and served as deputy team leader of the 1973 Mariner 10 Venus-Mercury robot flyby. Those were the halcyon days of NASA, the fulfillment of some of my most heartfelt dreams, expressed collectively in love, joy, excitement, and magnificent achievement.

Then things went downhill. During the 1970s, I felt both NASA's external budget cuts and its in-house reprisals for my honest but pessimistic testimony before Congress on the potential difficulties of the proposed space shuttle. I went through my divorce. And I became disillusioned with academic politics as I wandered from university to university looking for the ideal environment, each time thinking I had found it only to discover later I hadn't. I even spent a few months working as an issues staffer on Morris Udall's presidential campaign only to discover the effects of burnout and the trappings of political greed for the White House (among the staffers, not Udall, who was exhausted most of the time). I realized that process and appearance axiomatically overwhelmed substance near the pinnacles of power. I retreated from the political scene with my personal life in shambles. It was soon after that when I had my awakening that spring morning at the Lifespring training in Philadelphia.

During the 1980s, I re-awakened to my childhood dreams and re-experienced the optimism of the sixties. I began to meditate, reach inside, and accept the world as it was. I began to learn that those of us working in the military-industrial complex were not bad people. We were simply players of an old game, acknowledgeably the only game in aerospace that offered significant money. Deep down, most of my colleagues would rather be working on going to Mars with the Soviets than building space weapons. For technocrats, then, the coming conversion *should* be easy—simply work on new Mars contracts instead of old Star Wars contracts! Go to where the money has shifted.

Since I didn't have the heart to work on Star Wars, where most of the action was, there was little work left for me. The NASA space station changed concept and leadership so often it became a chimera. I left in early 1987, essentially to fall off the proverbial cliff into self-employment.

Three Levels of Behavior

Based on my first-hand experience with NASA, government, and politics in general, I propose there are three levels of behavior operant in today's world. The first is the old game, with the center of action being the political system such as it is, the dominance of the military-industrial complex in decision making, and the ever-growing, intricate money-manipulating infrastructure that feeds on it all, amplified by the mass media which has taken over even the dead shell of religion. Profit for profit's sake and material comforts are the major surface motivating factors. Beneath all this is fear—of the Russians, of no money, of death, etc. Most people are playing the old game because they are not consciously aware of any alternative. Even if alternatives were broached, they do not believe them to be realistic because of the underlying fear mechanism and a perceived threat to their material comforts. We are enmeshed in massive denial. The emotions of primitive fear and greed pervade the old game.

The second phase is what I call the protest game. This begins when a significant proportion of the population becomes disillusioned with the status quo. Motivated by anger, the protesters often create change by revolution, sometimes bloody. When a country is structurally strong enough, such as the United States, the change can come peacefully, letting the old order die of its own ineptitude. This is what happened to the war in Vietnam. The only problem with protest itself is that what replaces the old is usually just as corrupt—a wolf in new clothing. For example, we have Reagan's and Bush's all-time-high peacetime military budget, governmental-industrial revolving doors, pork barrelling, and covert foreign military aid, instead of a bloody war in someone else's domain.

While the anger and indignation of outsiders can temporarily call attention to the apparently outrageous activities of the old gamers, their effectiveness is limited and temporary. When the goals of the protestors are satisfied, they themselves usually become old gamers. Thus we see the war protestors of the sixties becoming the computer scientists and stockbrokers of the eighties. The Yippies become the Yuppies. Alternatively the institutions formed for the purpose of protesting a specific situation may stay intact after that problem is resolved, but institutional inertia and lack of purpose will inevitably send the institution itself back to playing the old game. Protest may be a good catalyst but it cannot maintain the needed changes. An individual who remains angry cannot sustain change. He is too busy being angry.

What we have left is a third mode of behavior: the new game or the new reality. This, too, is played out of moral conviction, but from a disciplined space of expressing itself positively toward all things and all people—even our "adversaries." Some people define this positive action as simply "loving." It is one thing to acknowledge the bitter truths of our time. It is another to remove the blame and anger, and proceed out of loving. Time and again, masters on this planet, going back to the times of Jesus and Buddha and before, have taught the simple truth of loving. The choice is ours, they say, to act out of fear, anger or loving. But only loving—real disciplined loving from the heart, not altruism or superficial sentimentality—will dissolve the negativity and bring lasting change to us as individuals and as societies. Anger may catalyze change, but only love consummates it. This does not mean the idea of love; it means the practice of love. Learning this is even more difficult than learning to be an astronaut.

But it works! I have found it to be subtle, yet very powerful. I can walk into a political leader's office without a specific agenda of either supporting an old game concept or supporting a protest concept. In fact, often all I need to do is to have a loving attitude, propose positive solutions to problems, and speak from my heart in the moment. What I have discovered from personal experience is that when I do this everybody else in the room seems to attempt to do the same thing, and the fear and anger appear to dissolve.

These techniques seem to work regardless of religious beliefs or philosophical outlooks. In Chapter 7, we will see how the effects of such a loving consciousness can even be measured by dowsing rods, suggesting that there is a scientific reality at work, not just an abstract concept.

I must admit I am only learning this technique. I suspect that making love real is the largest challenge facing those of us associated with the peace movement. A part of me is still angry. I not only acknowledge the inequities and cruelties of the old game, I also feel deprived by them. I am angry with American leaders for failing to grasp the opportunities. I am angry with the media for reporting only disaster, scandals, and distractions from peace. I am sometimes angry with the money-manipulating infrastructure for pocketing the profits of military-industrial gaming. I am also sometimes angry with my academic, industrial and governmental professional colleagues for "selling out."

Citizen Diplomacy

Along with others, I am beginning to realize that my anger is part of an illusion of separation and that it must be released before entering our new world view. What may be most surprising about this exciting new development is that the leadership role does not rest primarily on governments, industries and universities in the Western world. The leaders instead are citizen diplomats, principally from the United States and the Soviet Union, who have had the direct experience of cross-cultural contact from the heart. Our perceived differences dissolve when we experience such contact. We are discovering in our hearts that the externalization of our passion for peace is happening more rapidly than our minds can conceive.

Indeed, world peace is a reflection of inner peace. To the extent that we work as individuals to come to that quiet place inside, we are finding peace achievable in groups, communities, countries, and now on the entire planet. Isn't it ironic that the two most heavily armed superpower nations, which for more than a generation have been capable of annihilating the planet, now have citizens who are taking this leadership role? Our inner growth processes are paying off in the collective consciousness of the Earth.

As many of you probably do, I still find myself sometimes

hanging suspended between anger and loving. I am seeking a patient, tolerant attitude that accepts that somehow universal order will prevail and that I will make the right decisions at the right times. I ask myself: In terms of political and social consciousness, what is my real purpose?

In January 1988 I traveled to Moscow to talk with my cosmonaut friends and scientist colleagues about the prospects of a joint manned mission to Mars. I discovered that, not only are they interested in doing this, they want it done as soon as possible and as a replacement for nuclear and space weapons programs. I found more friends sharing this thought over there than I had here! They intend to translate my book *Mars 1999* into Russian and print 100,000 copies. And in some of those special non-verbal moments we experience with another human being I was able to meet with Russians in a place of open hearts. Again, if this was deception, the deception was so powerful as to transform us both. Our distrust dissolved into the illusion that was the past.

The Japanese are also interested in going to Mars. They too have translated and published *Mars 1999* and have formed a consortium of business and political leaders to promote the concept. Part of the new reality is Japan's emergence as the world technological leader, while the Americans and Soviets correspondingly squander precious resources on weapons of massive destruction. A recent meeting I had with both Japanese and Russian space leaders shows we can at least conceptually work together and synergize new space and Earth agendas.

By this point, most scientific and political colleagues have given up on me as a co-worker and I have given up on them as my support system. I am no longer an old game insider. I could not find in these people the proper context to express my enthusiasm. They displayed no openness to new ideas. I grieve the loss.

But, I found an entirely new vehicle for expression at the Soviet-American Citizens Summit held in Washington D.C. in February, 1988, a support system more powerful than I had ever dreamed. Teaming with my Soviet cosmonaut counterparts, I discovered we could create results (proposed new legislation) neither of us could create acting alone.

It was also there that I met several new American friends whose thinking was similar to mine and who were also ready to move with their training to support world transformation through releasing the fear and anger that have held us hostage to the old order and its illusionary reality. My purpose at last had been given its true definition: I am to lovingly express to others the application of new thought to individual experience and to world affairs. I am to express concrete projects as metaphors for the forthcoming transformation—for example, the mission to Mars. I am to share the kind of ideas expressed in this book. The awe I had experienced as a boy is now being consummated in an unexpected way. I invite you to join me in linking humankind's greatest adventures: exploring inner and outer space in harmony with our brothers and sisters on Earth.

Love and peace are the principal qualities that open our hearts to exploring the new reality. If we are too cynical, we will miss its essence. That is why I have needed to tell my story the way I have, including the expression of the political context of which we are all a part. The daily functioning of most of the planet is still enmeshed in illusion. We can embrace it all lovingly as our very matrix and yet move beyond it into the new reality. In Chapter 4 we shall see how the peaceful international exploration of outer space provides the ideal metaphor for exploring the riches of inner space. For many of us, it will be our passport into the new consciousness.

3

THE NEW PHYSICS

> The most beautiful thing we can experience is the mysterious. It is the source of all true art and science.
>
> —Albert Einstein

I majored in physics in college because I wanted to explore the mysteries of space. The timing couldn't have been more perfect. The launching of Sputnik, on October 4, 1957, marked the beginning of my freshman year at Williams College. Almost half the freshman class flooded into the lecture hall to take the mathematically intensive Physics 1A. The nation needed scientists and engineers fast and we were answering the collective call!

As I dug deeper into my field, I found the work to be time-consuming and difficult. The number of physics majors dropped dramatically from about 125 to 25. I barely hung in with Cs, improving to As only in graduate school. My space dream almost came true when I was appointed as a NASA astronaut. Alas, budget cuts dampened the promise of a space flight, so I returned to academia.

But my schooling and the years of research to follow were not in vain. I felt I truly had a grasp of how things worked, from the toaster oven to the Apollo Saturn rocket. The mechanical and chemical universe was my oyster. It was no longer a mystery, save for predicting the descriptive aspects of as yet unknown places, such as the Martian surface. I learned that a relatively small number of immutable laws such as that of gravity covered just about everything everywhere. Even the distant galaxies and stars obeyed gravity and were found to be made largely of the same material that comprise the major bodies of our solar system: hydrogen.

I learned that our common range of outer experience as humans on Earth can be readily explained by the laws of classical mechanics first articulated by Newton more than three centuries ago. This world-view encompasses a reality which we envision as solid bodies that move and interact predictably and repeatedly in a rigid framework of space and time in which the observer is independent of the observed.

In this view, matter can be reduced into fundamental solid building blocks called atoms. These chunks of matter should behave as billiard balls moving through space under strict laws which determine precisely where we can find them in the past and future. Electricity and magnetism did not become understood until the nineteenth century, but then they too involved laws and principles akin to those of classical mechanics. Charged particles such as electrons generate a field and move through conductors.

These models were drastically challenged early this century by the theories and experiments of relativity and quantum mechanics. In relativity, observations of objects moving near the speed of light reveal distortions in our measurement of space, time, and mass. The mathematics of relativity shows the counterintuitive result that an observer travelling near the speed of light will experience a shorter elapsed time than that measured by a stationary observer. In quantum mechanics, we do not find tiny building blocks but instead an ambiguous wave/particle duality of atomic systems which are irrevocably disturbed by the act of observation. Quantum theory underlies virtually every modern invention from electronics to nuclear weapons.

Interestingly, the full import of the new physics did not begin to strike me until the 1970s. In the safety of the physics department offices, I had been used to teaching the key equations, using the appropriate language, and playing my part as a rational spokesman even for the seemingly irrational, counter-intuitive and bizarre aspects of the new physics. In short, I had really lived my life relating to mechanical cause-and-effect, predictable billiard ball thinking, as most of us do. Because the mechanistic view of reality is so reinforced in our everyday experience of the five senses, we shall see in this book that the newer realities of physics and the paranormal are often ignored or denied, hidden in detached, intellectual exercises of mathematics, model building, and the discovery of new particles.

Scientists often forget their true purpose: to explore, to build models, to explain how things work, and to describe as simply and elegantly as possible principles that apply to a wide range of phenomena. When scientists think they have all the answers, when they demand proof in a totally controlled and repeatable experiment (even to consider the existence of a possible new reality), when they deny the reality of phenomena they don't want to confront, or when they attempt to explain with authority why a certain law of the universe must apply, they are quite out of their league.

It was not until after my 1977 workshop experience—an event my physicist friends would have found blasphemous, irrelevant, and even the act of a disturbed and lost soul—that I began to open myself to the true significance of the new physics. I suddenly realized that the new physics must not only embrace the very tiny (quantum mechanics) or the very fast or dense (relativity). It also needs to examine how we can communicate our consciousness across space and time. My mind still vacillates from belief to disbelief as that part of me that is rational and scientifically trained struggles against the irrational implications of my experience.

The new physics is a powerful scientific gateway to the paranormal: it is the most direct Western path to mysticism. It provides a more acceptable framework for some highly unusual phenomena that we will be examining in later chapters.

What is it about the new physics that so opens our minds and hearts to the new reality? Many writers have lucidly expressed the linkage between the new physics and mystical experiences. My purpose in writing this book is not to go over these perspectives and concepts again but to apply their findings to the new reality. Here we are talking about more than the mysteries of quantum physics and relativity; we are talking about "paraphysics," the physics of consciousness itself. The physics-paraphysics relationship was also well known to the pioneers of quantum mechanics—Bohr, Pauli, Heisenberg, and Shroedinger, to name just a few.

It is unfortunate that often the only new-reality vestige remaining from the early work in the physics classroom is the quantitative information and deductive aspects of quantum theory. Meanwhile, the physics-metaphysics parallels present major obstacles to researchers and teachers who continue to view reality in a detached, mechanistic, reductionistic manner.

One of my most challenging tasks in writing this book has been to understand the many levels of complexity of the new physics and to explain them in a way that can be understood by the uninitiated reader. Because of the heavy use of mathematics and new concepts involved, a brief chapter cannot do it justice. Still I can summarize the major findings and ask your forbearance if you find some ideas hard to grasp.

In order to recapture the essence of the new physics from its early discoveries, we must look at the observations coming from some of its pioneers. Perhaps no idea has more reshaped physics than Heisenberg's uncertainty principle, first expressed in 1927, which states that we cannot simultaneously pinpoint the location and motion of a particle/wave. Such a principle could be reduced to triviality if we didn't have the observers and apparatus to find this out—but we do. It is simply a fact that, at the subatomic level, the observer interferes with the observed and so any number of outcomes is possible. There can be no predetermination, no more reduction of matter to ultimate building blocks. Any predictability in quantum mechanics comes only from the statistics of ensembles of large numbers of particles/waves. But the individual particle/wave enters into an unpredictable dance with the observer-participant.

"One extreme is the idea of an objective world," wrote Werner Heisenberg, "pursuing its regular course in space and time, independently of any kind of observing subject; this has been the guiding image from modern science. At the other extreme is the idea of a subject, mystically experiencing the unity of the world and no longer confronted by an object or by any objective world; this has been the guiding image of Asian mysticism. Our thinking moves somewhere in the middle, between these two limiting conceptions we should maintain the tensions resulting from these opposites."

Books have been written about the application of this one principle to our understanding of consciousness and mysticism. Perhaps the most bizarrely speculative is *Stalking the Wild Pendulum* by Itzhak Bentov, who proposes that when matter reaches a moment of rest (for example, when a pendulum reaches the farthest point in its swing) its position spreads into the universe to embrace infinite space, infinite awareness, infinite consciousness. At that precise moment, while we have pinpointed the speed of the pendulum to be zero, we have allowed its location to instantaneously spread to encompass all reality. This principle could apply to our own consciousness as well, at those turning-point moments when our breath moves from inhaling to exhaling to inhaling. This is consistent with the experience of many mystics.

"Really deep concepts seem to take fifty years to sink into the collective conscience of the thinking community," according to the molecular biophysicist Harold Morowitz. "So it is that only now are most of us beginning to sense the full impact of certain ideas that have been brewing in physics since the first quarter of this century." The new physics is just now finding a secure home while the paranormal remains on the outside knocking to come in. But it is not far behind.

How far have the modern physicists gone and where do they draw the line between what they accept as reality and what they are afraid to address? In physics, the big task appears to boil down to bringing together the four observed forces of nature into a single unified field theory. Albert Einstein had attempted to do this in his later years and failed. Many physicists today are at work on this same problem.

The four forces consist of gravity, electromagnetic forces, the weak nuclear force (radioactive decay) and the strong nuclear force (which binds the nucleus of an atom). A unified field theory would combine quantum mechanics, gravity and relativity and "should resolve all the mysteries left unsolved," according to the legendary cosmologist Stephen Hawking, author of the recently published best-seller, *A Brief History of Time*. Hawking feels the momentous day of discovery is not far off.

According to some physicists, mathematical reconciliation between the forces occurs when all matter and energy is conceived of as vibrating strings in ten dimensional space. This is appropriately enough called string theory. While the mathematical consistency is striking, critics have difficulty envisioning ten dimensions, six of which are so tiny they are hidden from view (the other four include the familiar three of space and one of time). It is like being a hypothetical two-dimensional being on a flat world insisting that a sphere is a circle.

Hawking, a brilliant scientist whose mind remarkably transcends the crippling effects of Lou Gehrig's disease, is one of the leading optimists about reconciling the laws of physics. In his book, he takes us on an intellectual journey through the wonders of the universe. He shows us the limits of space-time in terms of exotic theoretical places like singularities, black holes, and the state of the universe at the time of its hypothesized "big bang" origin. Black holes are objects that are so dense that, according to Einstein's theory of general relativity, time and space collapse on themselves and the laws of physics as we know them break down inside.

But Hawking remains undaunted. "When we combine quantum mechanics and general relativity," he writes, "there seems to be a new possibility that did not exist before: that space and time together might form a finite, four-dimensional space without singularities or boundaries, like the surface of the earth but with more dimensions. It seems that this idea could explain many of the observed features of the universe, such as its large-scale uniformity and also the smaller-scale departures from homogeneity, like galaxies, stars and even human beings. It could even account for the arrow (direction) of time that we observe. Yet if the universe is completely described by a unified theory, that has profound implications for the role of God as creator . . . it would be the ultimate triumph of human reason—for then we would know the mind of God."

As brilliant as Hawking's analysis may be and as all-encompassing the range of observations he may have considered, *as seen from the perspective of the physicist*, there exist a wide body of data he has ignored. These involve the paranormal, the mind, and human consciousness. I believe we cannot know the mind of God through knowing the laws of orthodox physics alone, no matter how brilliantly we conceive and reconcile them.

The new physics introduces innovative concepts and principles that broaden our perspective of our new world view. But we shall see that these observations are not enough. They help remind us that our mechanistic thinking has its limitations. They point us in the right direction, but we're by no means all the way there. We are still within orthodoxy.

Some brave physicists have gone further than Hawking. For example, Alan Guth of MIT has recently proposed that in using wormholes, theoretical holes in time and space that permit instantaneous tunneling to distant parts of the universe, "it would be apparently possible for an advanced society literally to create an entirely new universe." Here we are closer to a scientific redefinition of the relation between mind and matter. But we are still among professional scientists who have not taken into account the internal mysteries of their lives. You cannot envision the secrets of the whole (holistic, holographed) universe from a think tank, between lunch and dinner.

In his book *Star Wave*, Fred Allen Wolf argues that the principles of quantum physics translate directly to consciousness. "If quantum mechanics is taken literally, " he writes, "then time is unobservable and . . . parallel universes exist. . . . In our new age the role of mind predominates. . . . The mind may not exist in the physical universe at all. It may be beyond the boundaries of space, time, and matter. It may use the physical body in the same sense that an automobile driver uses a car . . ."

In November 1977, a group of innovative physicists met in Reykjavik, Iceland, to discuss the physics of consciousness. In this remarkable collection of articles collected in one volume, *The Iceland Papers*, the physicists applied the well-known results of quantum theory to such paranormal phenomena as precognition, psychokinesis, and telepathy. Physicists Richard Mattuck and Evan Walker, along with Fred Allen Wolf, posit a "collapse of the quantum wave function" of materials subjected to the concentration of psychics and clairvoyants. The result is the distortion and transformation, towards what we do not yet know, of our familiar concepts of time, space, and matter.

Quantum mechanics, which has made possible television, miniature electronics, computers, nuclear energy, and lasers, may also help pave the way to our understanding of the principles of mind and awareness.

One prime example is the hologram—a three-dimensional image created by the interference of light waves sent from a laser. Anyone who has gone through the haunted house at Disneyland or Disney World has seen some realistic but wispy-looking holograms. The hologram has the curious property of indestructibility. Shatter the image, and instead of seeing it break into pieces, you see several dimmer renditions of the same image. Similarly, some scientists believe that the brain does not appear to consist of specialized units that perform mechanical tasks like a computer, but is a complex, interconnected system in which each small part contains or reflects information about the whole. Could it also not be true that our minds are really replicas of a universal mind hypothesized by philosophers and spiritual leaders?

Within the context of studying quantum physics and consciousness, the ideas of time-space, matter, reductionism and mechanical causality begin to lose meaning. Instead, in the realm of new physics, we deal with concepts of energy, resonance, synchronicity and unity. In a unique collaboration, physicist Wolfgang Pauli and psychologist Carl Jung proposed that a given individual's or culture's view of physical-psychological reality could be expressed in the form of a location on a graph whose extremes would be causality and synchronicity on a horizontal axis, and indestructible energy and the space-time continuum on a vertical axis.

Until the twentieth century, the Western approach has rigidly hung on to the extremes of causality and space-time, but now that bubble has been irrevocably burst. In the new physics, mind meets matter, East meets West, yin meets yang, psychology meets physics, and mathematics meets mysticism. We are inevitably pulled toward the middle of the graph where we begin to understand the myths, metaphors, and practices of the mystical traditions of the Far East at the same time that we reach into the laws of matter. Heisenberg was a true prophet of this.

Many books written over a decade ago describe the profound Eastern connection to modern physics: *The Tao of Physics* by physicist Fritjof Capra, *The Dancing Wu Li Masters* by Gary Zukav, and *Mysticism and The New Physics* by Michael Talbot.

"Science does not need mysticism and mysticism does not need science," Capra concluded, "but man needs both. Mystical experience is necessary to understand the deepest nature of things, and science is essential for modern life. . . . At present our attitude is too yang—too rational, male, and aggressive. Scientists themselves are a typical example. Although their theories are leading to a world-view which is similar to that of the mystics, it is striking how little this has affected the attitudes of most scientists."

Talbot's book is well-documented with regard to the commonality he proposes between the physicists' findings and the insights of some of the great Eastern and Western thinkers of our time. "The convergence of mysticism and the new physics has brought us to the gateway of our humanness," Talbot concludes. "Beyond it lies something that is literally beyond our language. In the words of Satprem, 'We are at the beginning of the 'Vast' which will always be vaster . . . the physical world itself will change soon before our incredulous eyes.'"

Talbot sees no death of physics, only transformation. "Perhaps when the scientific establishment at large realizes that the puzzles encountered in psychic phenomena are already part of the very fabric of science, serious research efforts can begin. Indeed, in light of Wheeler's notion of the role of the 'participation,' physics may have to invent psychic research, if it did not already exist."

The Paranormal

We cannot scientifically deny the reality of many paranormal experiences and experiments (e.g., consciousness communication, psychic insights, psychokinesis, synchronicity, out-of-body experiences, etc.) any more than we can deny the observations of quantum physics and relativity. There are too many unmistakable results that preclude even the remote possibility that they are *all* hoaxes or illusions. I believe that paranormal research is at a similar stage to quantum physics and relativity in the early twentieth century.

Just as Einstein, Heisenberg, Bohr, Pauli, and their colleagues were stunned at the counterintuitive nature of their observations, many of us are having difficulty making sense of the paradoxical relation of mind over matter. Yet these pioneers persevered through the adverse criticism of their peers and persisted to the end in their search for the truth. They didn't *want* the results they were getting. And so it goes for the paranormal. There is an uneasy excitement in the air.

Those of us involved in paranormal research can learn a lesson from quantum physics and relativity. We can take those observations we know to be valid and develop some operating principles underlying those observations. The new physics at first involved a few principles, some of which later became well-established theories. Heisenberg's uncertainty principle, the holographic brain model, and participant-observer principles are examples, but there are others.

We have the Pauli exclusion principle that permits only certain energy states for electrons. We have the anthropic principle which states that the universe is here because we are here; a randomly developing universe could not accommodate us. We have the matter-energy equivalence principle which states that matter is stored energy following the formula $E = mc^2$. We have Bell's Theorem which proposes that each of any two particles that have previously interacted "know" what the other is doing even after they separate.

How do these principles of physics apply to the paranormal? Do they apply only by analogy or is our everyday reality (encompassing both the normal and the paranormal) a direct consequence of the principles of the new physics? These points are debatable. Fred Alan Wolf is convinced that the mysteries of the mind can be solved through quantum physics. Nobel laureates John Wheeler and Eugene Wigner (colleagues of mine at Princeton before I broke away from them in my own search for the truth) also believe that quantum physics and consciousness are interrelated, though they are hardly advocates of paranormal research. I basically agree with Wheeler's and Wigner's view, although the paranormal cannot any longer be ignored.

We do not know for sure the degree to which the new physics maps the paranormal, but we can articulate some principles that seem to apply to certain categories of phenomena. In the chapters to follow I will describe experiences and experiments along with some underlying principles.

Because of the importance of observer participation, I am also proposing that we all need to be observers whenever possible. Direct experience transcends "the literature" as a reality test for each phenomenon. Suspending disbelief and being open to the experience appear to be important prerequisites to validating the experience; scientific work can proceed in its familiar environment after the relatively non-scientific nature of undergoing the personal experience itself. It is fortunate that, unlike the new physics, the paranormal is available to any of us. We do not need Ph.D.s, IQs over 150, a multi-billion dollar particle accelerator, or a ride into space.

Conclusion

In summary, the discoveries of the new physics in the early twentieth century were unexpected. They directly contradicted the laws of physics as we then knew them. They made no logical sense. And yet observation after observation, finding after finding, and invention after invention, confirm the power and potential of the new physics. By analogy, the current discoveries in a wide range of paranormal phenomena and individual transformative experience are forcing us to drop the old way of looking at things and to develop a new model of our reality. As parapsychologist Jule Eisenbud so succinctly put it, "All science is patent pending."

The new physics therefore points the way toward the first two major elements of our new reality: that all models, existing and new, are open to question and that our inner and outer space are constantly interacting. In the remainder of the book, we will address a third, more elusive but very important element: that our inner space profoundly influences our outer space and, in fact, the unity of all humankind.

Bibliography

Augros, Robert M. and George N. Stanciu, *The New Story of Science*, Gateway Editions, Lake Bluff, Illinois (1984).

Bentov, Itzhak, *Stalking the Wild Pendulum*, E.P. Dutton, New York (1975).

Capra, Fritjof, *The Tao of Physics*, Shambhala Publications, Boulder, CO (1975).

Capra, Fritjof, *The Turning Point*, Simon and Schuster, New York (1982).

Eisenbud, Jule, interview, p. 164 in *Ecology and Consciousness*, edited by Richard Grossinger, North Atlantic Books, Berkeley, Calf. (1978).

Hawking, Stephen, *A Brief History of Time*, Bantam, New York (1988).

Heisenberg, Werner, *Across the Frontier*, Harper & Row, New York (1974).

The Iceland Papers, edit. by Andrija Puharich, Essentia Research Associates, Amherst, Wisconsin (1979).

Jung, Carl and Wolfgang Pauli, *The Interpretation of Nature and the Psyche*, Bollingen Series LI, Pantheon Books, New York (1967).

Lemonick, Michael D., "Wormholes in the Heavens," *Time*, January 16, 1989, p. 55.

Morowitz, Harold, *The Wine of Life and Other Essays on Societies, Energy and Living Things*, St. Martin's, New York (1979).

Satprem, *Sri Aurobindo or the Adventure of Consciousness*, Harper & Row, New York (1969).

Talbot, Michael, *Mysticism and The New Physics*, Bantam, New York (1980).

Toben, Bob, *Space-Time and Beyond*, Dutton, New York (1975).

Wolf, Fred Allen, *Star Wave*, Collier, New York (1986).

Zukav, Gary, *The Dancing Wu Li Masters*, Morrow, New York (1979).

4

THE INNER-OUTER SPACE CONNECTION

> The voyages into outer space turn us back to inner space . . . It's fashionable now to demand some economic payoff from space, some reward to prove it was all worthwhile. Those who say this resemble the apelike creatures in *2001*. They are fighting for food among themselves, while one separates himself from them and moves to the slab, motivated by awe. That is the point they are missing. He is the one who evolves into a human being; he is the one who understands the future . . . the fear of the unknown, this free-fall into the future can be detected all around us. But we live in the stars and we are finally moved by awe to our greatest adventures. The Kingdom of God is within us. And Easter and Passover remind us that we have to let go in order to enter it.
>
> —Joseph Campbell

While the mind-boggling concepts of the new physics provide an intellectually palatable entree into the new reality, in the end only our own experiences will provide the necessary reality tests. Mathematical equations depicting ten-dimensional strings and quarks do not engage the interested layperson. Exploring inner and outer space does, and it provides an opportunity to participate rather than just hypothesize.

To those of us who are old enough to remember, Neil Armstrong's and Buzz Aldrin's first steps on the Moon on July 20, 1969 were an extraordinary experience not only for the two astronauts but for two billion people on Earth identifying with them on television. For a few brief minutes, the planet came together in consciousness celebrating perhaps the greatest physical feat in recorded human history.

The significance of the first human footprints on the Moon went far, far beyond a particular historic experience. It marked, as Joseph Campbell said, a time in which our ignorance and complacency were coming to an end. The image of Earthrise over the lunar horizon, observed by the lunar orbiting astronauts, did not signify a new cosmology, but it signified a new phenomenology. Things would never be the same.

The view of the whole planet Earth from space symbolizes a birth of consciousness. As the astronauts gazed down on our seemingly colored marble in the black sea, they were transformed. The spectacular photographs they brought back, which probably adorn the walls of more offices and homes than any other category of picture, remind us poignantly that we have one very beautiful fragile planet to love and to preserve. Our experience *is* a unity.

More than any single event or symbol, we can thank the existence of a single photograph of the whole Earth for the genesis of the ecology movement of the 1970s and our growing awareness that our war making and polluting must be reversed. Breaking the precedent of a man or woman of the year, *Time* designated the Earth as *planet* of the year for 1988.

The Experiences of Astronauts

The evidence is abundant that the exploration of outer space, barely one human generation old, is a major catalyst for planetary transformation. Exploring outer space becomes a metaphor for exploring inner space and achieving the seeming unachievable: planetary consciousness and harmony. That is one reason going to Mars has such dramatic potential.

Author Frank White calls this the "overview effect." Interviewing or reviewing the writings of twenty-four astronauts and cosmonauts that have taken the trip into space, White concludes that the human presence in space not only transforms the individual, it transforms the world. White cites the value of "central projects" such as the Egyptian pyramids, the great cathedrals, and the Apollo project. These projects, according to Willis Harman and Howard Rheingold, "attract the best and most adventurous minds of the age ... (They) educate the consciousness of the larger population . . . (and are a) means of focusing the energies of a population during an evolutionary transition to a higher level of culture."

White concludes that, "My research on the Overview Effect suggests that it is merely a warm-up for space exploration's potential role as the greatest cultural project in human history . . . The Overview Effect and related phenomena are the foundations for a series of new civilizations evolving on Earth and in space." We are living in a time possibly no less radical and profound than when our first fish ancestors crawled onto land: humans are about to evolve into space.

Astronaut Rusty Schweickart eloquently described his view of the Earth from orbit—a rapidly moving landscape, cloudscape and oceanscape in which he circled the globe in 90 minutes, traveling silently and weightlessly at the staggering speed of five miles per second. He began to identify with familiar places like Los Angeles and Phoenix and Houston, and then with less familiar places like North Africa.

"And that whole process of what it is you identify with begins to shift," he said. "When you go around the Earth for an hour and a half, you begin to recognize that your identity is with that whole thing. That makes a change. You look down there and you can't imagine how many borders and boundaries you cross, again and again and again, and you don't even see them. There you are—hundreds of people in the Mideast killing each other over some imaginary line that you're not even aware of and that you can't see.

"From where you see it, the thing is a whole, and it's so beautiful. You wish you could take one in each hand, one from each side in the various conflicts, and say, 'Look. Look at it from this perspective. Look at that. What's important?'

"Then you look back on the time you were outside on the EVA (extra-vehicular activity or space walk) and on those few moments that you could take, because a camera malfunctioned, to think about what was happening. And you recall staring out there at the spectacle that went before your eyes, because you're no longer inside something with a window, looking out at a picture. Now you're out there and there are no frames, there are no limits, there are no boundaries. You're really out there, going twenty-five thousand miles an hour, ripping through space, a vacuum. And there's not a sound. There's a silence the depth of which you've never experienced before, and that silence contrasts so markedly with the scenery you're seeing and the speed with which you know you're moving.

"You think about what you're experiencing and why. Do you deserve this, this fantastic experience? Have you earned this in some way? Are you separated out to be touched by God, to have some special experience that others cannot have? You know that the answer to that is no. There's nothing that you've done that deserves that, that earned that; it's not a special thing for you. You know very well at that moment, and it comes through to you so powerfully that you're the sensing element for man. You look down and see the surface of that globe that you've lived on all this time, and you know all those people down there and they are like you, they are you—and somehow you represent them.

"You are up there as the sensing element, that point out on the end, and that's a humbling feeling. It's a feeling that says you have a responsibility. It's not for yourself. The eye that doesn't see doesn't do justice to the body. That's why it's there; that's why you are out there.

"And somehow you recognize that you're a piece of this total life . . . You're out there on the forefront and you have to bring that back somehow. That becomes a rather special responsibility and it tells you something about your relationship with this thing we call life. So that's a change. That's something new. And when you come back there's a difference in the world now. There's a difference in that relationship between you and that planet and you and all those other forms of life on that planet, because you've had that kind of experience. It's a difference and it's so precious.

"And all through this I've used the word you because it's not me, it's not Dave Scott, it's not Dick Gordon, Pete Conrad, John Glenn—it's you, it's we. It's Life that's had the experience."

In his journey to the Moon on Apollo 14, astronaut Ed Mitchell had a transformative experience. "Spaceflight is one of the more powerful experiences that humans can have," he told Frank White, "and the technological event of breaking the bonds of Earth is far more important that the technology that went into it . . .

"Spaceflight, getting outside of Earth and seeing it from a different perspective, having this sort of explosive awareness that some of us had, this abiding concern and passion for the well-being of Earth . . . will have a direct impact on philosophy and value systems. It's got to be investigated far more thoroughly."

Mitchell and White also found that the interpretation of the outer space experience varies enormously from astronaut to astronaut. This interpretation depends largely on the individual's belief system. They found that the largest variable in measuring the overview effect is not an outer space parameter such as the whole Earth or weightlessness. It is the astronaut himself. This leads us to a third element of our greater new reality: our inner space profoundly affects our outer space. We have already seen from the new physics the first two elements: that no one model of reality is sacred and that we are all interconnected.

Mitchell went on to found the Institute of Noetic Sciences, an organization dedicated to the investigation of the relationship of science and consciousness. Schweickart founded the Association of Space Explorers, a group of astronauts and cosmonauts seeking the brotherhood and sisterhood of mankind. We see in both astronauts' missions a persistent desire to create global harmony and a yearning for a broader scientific paradigm. "The payoff from Apollo may be estimably richer than anyone anticipated," Mitchell concluded.

On a sadder note, Mitchell reflected on the view of the Earth he had from the Moon. Being able to blot out the Earth with his thumb, he mused: "The crew of spacecraft Earth is in virtual mutiny to the order of the universe." He felt himself to be more a planetary citizen than a United States citizen.

The more we master the physical universe, said Buckminster Fuller, the more prepared we are to transform to higher consciousness. By mastery, Fuller intends a peaceful coexistence with the Earth, not the sort of exploitation, weaponization and pollution that could wipe us out. Schweickart and Mitchell well represent those values as ambassadors in space.

My Entree to Inner-Outer Space

My mother recalls how I geared all my school projects toward becoming an astronaut and exploring space. I remember the night at Harvard Observatory when I was eight looking at Saturn through the telescope and the astronomer explaining to me that this exotic ringed world was bigger than planet Earth and was more than a billion miles away! In one instant I transformed.

Outer space became inner space through an act akin to Eureka!

But my teachers felt I was unrealistic; after all, in 1948 there was no space program. They thought, at best, I could become a geriatric astronaut in the twenty-first century. In the spring of 1957, our high school history teacher asked us to write an essay on an important contemporary topic. I wrote mine on space satellites. He handed it back with the comment, "Well researched but not relevant." The following fall, Sputnik went up, and only ten years later I was to be appointed as the nation's second youngest astronaut of the Apollo program, too "junior" to take the trip into space. A couple of years later man landed on the Moon.

Somehow as a child I sensed the deeper meaning of space exploration. With the benefit of hindsight, I now see it as a transposed metaphor for exploring inner space. It is the central technology project of our time that will catalyze us to the ultimate frontier of consciousness.

Problems in Linking Inner and Outer Space

Two apparent problems come up regarding the outer space-inner space connection. The first is that exploring inner space is not a central project. It does not get international publicity nor does our language have words to adequately describe the experience. It is the ultimate decentralized project, and that is why so many of us are dissuaded from its benefits.

The second problem is that we do not now have an outer-space central project analogous to Apollo to inspire humanity towards the new reality which includes the integration of both outer- and inner-space exploration. An international Mars mission by 2000, or comparably bold goal, could fulfill the "outer space" need. Or, as we shall see in Chapter 6, a possible release of information regarding contacts with extraterrestrial beings or a potential dramatic revelation of their presence could preempt even the plans of visionary leaders. The existence of such beings may bring outer and inner space together.

Meanwhile, we will need to be satisfied with metaphors and models of how positive uses of outer space can educate us into higher consciousness. Outer space in many ways serves the same purpose as the new physics: it provides a physical pathway into the new reality.

Physical Metaphors for Inner Space

In mystical teachings we hear references to energy levels, vibratory rates, the pull of gravity, the finiteness of our planet, and reflected light versus radiated light. All of these concepts have their origin and analogues in physics and space science, which have their origin, in turn, in alchemical and occult science. Without access to these analogues, it would be difficult to understand what is happening to us in our inner being.

We inhabit a mental world during most of our waking hours. Even this book is a mental approach to the experiential domain. In my opinion, science awaits a renaissance in exploring the huge grey area between the current practice of the objective natural sciences and the unlimited vistas of the participatory spiritual cosmos. Mediating between are various yet interrelated components such as experiencing weightlessness in outer space, studying paranormal phenomena, and other frontiers of science, searching for extraterrestrial intelligence, evolving off our planet, viewing and contemplating the whole Earth, and considering theories of our planet evolving toward a superorganism of four billion humans.

In spiritual teachings we often hear of reflected light and radiated light, about the light side and the dark side. The same is true in the physical sciences, yet rarely are the two ideas adequately expressed together.

Spiritually-oriented people often want to know more about how physical processes can shed more light on their inner experiences. Scientists often want to know how their findings can be extended into a broader range of experience. With open minds we find that the scientific and spiritual approaches reinforce each other.

Understanding and experiencing physical metaphors for spiritual realities go beyond the mental aspect. I have found that being able to visualize or experience something within me can be assisted enormously by understanding principles that apply to the physical universe. Conversely, my having an inner experience helps me visualize processes in the outer, physical universe that might lead to insights such as those I had in my planetary science days at Berkeley, Cornell and Princeton.

Radiated and Reflected Light

An example of how something in outer reality can be a metaphor for something in inner reality is the concept of radiated and reflected light. When my life is going well I experience a sensation of what-I-will-call radiating light. Feedback is reflected to me instantaneously, either in my own reflection or in the faces of others.

This radiated light is not emitted at visible frequencies nor detectable by the physical eye or a light meter. It emits an invisible frequency and is detectable by individuals who seem attuned to it.

Reflected light is easier to describe. It is simply the light of the sun or electric lights reflecting from a physical body. When we look at the Moon, Venus, Mars, Jupiter or other planets in the sky either with our naked eyes or through a telescope we are looking at reflected sunlight off the day side. That reflected component enables us to describe the appearance of their surfaces and make inferences about the planet's evolution—for example, meteor craters, mountains, windblown dust, etc. As in the case of reflected light off humans, reflected light off planets can be descriptive and interesting, but it tells us little about what is happening inside.

The celestial radiated component is a different story, again a close parallel with humans. We cannot detect any visible light radiated by planets with our eyes, but we can detect radiant light with instruments such as infrared detectors and radio telescopes. At visible frequencies the reflected component completely overwhelms the radiated component. At other frequencies the radiated component dominates. The radiated component also tells us what is happening inside, what is intrinsic to the planet, because it is energy that is being emitted from within the planet itself.

Some of the sunlight impinging on a planet's surface is reflected off into space and detectable at visible frequencies. The rest of it is absorbed into the planet and reradiated at other frequencies requiring instruments other than the eye to detect. The degree to which a planet reflects and radiates depends on its reflectivity. 100% reflectivity means a perfect white ball with no absorption or reradiation. 0% reflectivity means a pitch black object that you cannot see with your eyes but that absorbs and radiates perfectly at other frequencies. Moons and planets lie somewhere between. The Earth's Moon reflects only 6% of incident sunlight; the surface of the Earth reflects about 30%.

This doesn't mean people should wear black to radiate more light. It means that the radiating light within each of us is a manifestation of our inner reality or inner essence. The reflected light is descriptive of our physical body and because it is more easily visible, it tends to distract us from experiencing our inner life force.

Unlike inanimate objects, human beings can tap and radiate the invisible inner resources of "light." We have the potential to step up or step down our emitted light. Our inner source is not sunlight, or at least not three-dimensional sunlight, for the closer we get to the source, the more energy we seem to have available to radiate. It appears to radiate at all times in all directions. As we shall see in Chapter 7, its intensity and extent can be measured by dowsing rods. This "life force" is more like the power of faith healers or what is found in homeopathetic medicine.

Celestial Mechanics

Another physical or space metaphor for the new reality involves celestial mechanics, and was suggested to me by my colleague Dan Drasin. This branch of classical physics (invented by Isaac Newton) describes the motions of planets, satellites, planetary probes, the stars in our galaxy, and most of the physical universe. I learned it well in graduate school and taught it for many years at various universities.

The main expression of celestial mechanics is through the law of gravity. We all know about the effects of gravity. On Earth it is constantly pulling on us and its manifestations rule everyday life when we drop things, climb out of bed, jump, etc.

We also know that a trip into space is costly, about $10,000 a pound using the space shuttle. This is because we sit at the bottom of a gravity well, and our current technology is barely able to free us from the planet by means of huge chemical rockets.

But when we become free of gravity and escape the Earth, the scenario is totally different. Ninety years ago the Soviet rocket pioneer Konstantin Tsiolkovsky, and more recently, the American physicist Gerard O'Neill, pointed out the enormous economic advantage of operating in space free of terrestrial gravity. Instead, we can use the raw materials available to us in much smaller wells such as the Moon (twenty times less in energy required) and the asteroids (hundreds to thousands of times less). O'Neill suggested that soon humanity could evolve off this planet into space and create a self-sufficient industrial economy forever free of the Earth's pull. It makes pragmatic sense.

Having spent several years with O'Neill, I developed a variation of the theme that focuses on the resources of the tiny moons of Mars, Phobos, and Deimos. Not only could these become advantageous bases from which to explore Mars, they are gravitationally more accessible and resource-laden *even than our own Moon*! They probably contain large quantities of easily accessible water bound in the soil for refueling spacecraft and life support. Eventually we could have a self-supporting, Earth-independent human renaissance in space—asteroid mining, space colonies, solar power satellites, lunar and planetary bases, and star ships.

Imagine the transformative value of taking a journey to Mars in which the Earth recedes to a small disc, then to just another bright star. Imagine encountering signs of life having been on Mars.

How does all this relate to the new reality? I believe that we humans have been stuck in a consciousness gravity well. The old science of materialism and classical mechanics has bound us to a plane of ideas. We are not only trapped on the Earth's surface; we are trapped to the limiting beliefs of materialism. But mystic practice reminds us that we have another choice: we can build the rockets of inner space and travel the universe freely, not as a state project but as individual opportunities. Most of the rest of this book is a blueprint for doing this.

Once we have mastered the tools and have suspended disbelief, we will be on our way. Then we can travel to the Phoboses and Deimoses of inner space. Journeys out of the body described in Chapter 9 may be the most direct application of this aspect of the new reality.

Duality

Implied in this discussion is the duality of science and spirit, of probing the outer worlds and the inner worlds. We have all experienced feelings of duality in our lives: man and woman, right and wrong, negative and positive, good and bad, old vs. new paradigms. Many of our approaches to personal, social, and political situations reflect duality.

Our modern world is rife with duality. It permeates the Marxist dialectic, the capitalist win-lose, the Eastern Yin and Yang. Our legal adversarial system is a huge duality. The media promotes it by broadcasting the conflict and struggle on the physical level. Within education and religion there exists a duality between the "shoulds" we are given and the doubts with which we often react. Love itself becomes a duality of ideal and real.

Duality provides a mental reference system useful in expressing concepts. It's not important whether the duality exists out there as objectively real; it's what we make of our experience of duality that counts. In one sense it is an illusion of our own making, an artifact of our communication. There are times when we go about our lives observing the illusion of duality, while simultaneously experiencing a feeling of oneness and loving.

Other times we seem to be in the "thick of it." A poignant example is my own experience of communicating new concepts in space travel to my scientific colleagues while remaining true to my new reality values. Scientists and engineers generally require empirical data in order to embrace new concepts. New reality minds, however, often initially accept such ideas on either faith or personal experience only, which to some is scientifically unacceptable. The apparent conflict between these approaches creates duality. We are in need of "spiritual scientists," who are able to apply the scientific rigor without conditions.

In this book, I am working to span the gap of this duality, which at times appears to be a chasm. In the process, I am careful that what I say and do continually reflects my hard-earned credibility. I occasionally feel as though I am living in two worlds, like C.P. Snow's *Two Cultures* revisited. (C.P. Snow was a British scientist-writer who wrote this famous essay lamenting the separation and animosity between the scientists and humanists in England during the 1940s and 1950s.)

At times I create a duality within myself of "us" vs. "them." "Why do scientists need physical-level proof to make anything real," I ask myself, "when so many things independent of needing proof do happen?" Those are difficult times when I find myself playing the martyr and looking to blame others: I create my own duality.

Yin and Yang

We hear increasingly about the duality of yin and yang, the two polarities which, according to Oriental tradition, provide a mechanism for growth and eventual balance on the Earth. This ancient wisdom suggests that much of the evolution of the soul comes from resolving apparent conflicts between these two opposing forces.

Yin is the soft, feminine, receiving, nurturing energy on the planet. Yang is the hard, masculine, expressive, thrusting energy. The blending of yin and yang encompasses much more than sex, love, and marriage; it operates in virtually every imaginable human activity. Many philosophers believe that yin and yang interactions provide an elegant model for personal and social transformation.

We need the interplay of both polarities. Without sex, for example, we probably wouldn't survive for long—even with genetic engineering. And in our learning, without any ability to observe and experience duality, what would there be left to do or say? Without duality, much of our communication loses its impact. Through adversity, we grow and are transformed.

Women and men play the archetypal roles of yin and yang. Occasionally we get imbalances which, according to theories of cosmic law, will need redressing sooner or later. The dominance of any one polarity in any community or event becomes an eventual requirement for balancing action. The alternative to balancing is atrophy, diminished excitement, no real living or loving, the Swan Song, and ultimate death. History is full of examples of the results of these imbalances: wars, crusades, revolutions, slavery, prostitution, rape, murder, alcoholism, starvation, divorce, unequal pay, and the more strident aspects of women's liberation.

Aside from the fading influence of gentlemen's clubs and the Old Boy Network and parts of the military, I know of no more poignant example of the dominance of the yang forces nowadays than the exploration of space. In the early days we saw the yang of The Right Stuff. Men built and flew airplanes and rockets that thrust faster and higher to the edge of the atmosphere until they penetrated into space itself.

When I joined the U.S. Astronaut corps in 1967, there were 67 of us—all men. True, women have now been accepted into the program, but the aerospace field is still overwhelmingly yang. A walk down any NASA or contractor's corridor today immediately reveals yang energy in its full splendor: men in their plain cubby-holes, conference rooms with viewgraph machines and piles of paper rife with bullet charts and block diagrams, with an endless expression of acronyms and abbreviations. One time during a visit to Fairchild Aerospace's satellite production facility, I saw the brand name "Yang" on a huge lathe!

Even the popular space development groups are still predominantly male: before their recent merger, the L5 Society had twelve percent women and the National Space Institute was only six percent female.

But some curious things are beginning to happen. The next big project on NASA's drawing boards is the multimodular $16 billion space station, a permanent six to eight person facility that will begin to orbit in the late nineties. I suggest that the space station and destinations beyond will begin a manifestation of the yin forces, and we are in for a big shift in the space program starting in the 1990s.

By their very nature, space stations, lunar bases, and Mars bases are yin facilities. They are passive; they receive the rockets. And for the most part they don't do much besides just be there for months to years at a time while the data and rockets and people and equipment come and go. No longer the dynamic excitement of the grey cockpit with all those joy sticks and toggle switches and large noisy engine thrusters and pulling eight g's, the space stations of the future will quietly, benignly float (or be moored to a planet) like nests, while people work, live, sleep, and eat for months at a time.

During the 1990s, in one gigantic quantum leap, the total number of U.S. people-hours logged in space will go up twenty-fold. Are the "yangish" NASA engineers aware of the implications of this?

Probably not for now. The high-tech male crews still appear in the futuristic sketches, manipulating dials on marathon tasking in cramped quarters. Space station mockups at the Johnson Space Center and at McDonnell Douglas more resemble a locker room than a place to live. The cold, metallic high-tech look prevents astronauts who will spend over two hours a day on the exercise bike from even looking out the window.

Yet we get indications from the long Salyut and Skylab flights that space autonomy and the quest for privacy, the yearning for reflective viewing of the Earth and accommodating quarters, the turning off of radio chatter, and the muting of timelines dictated from the ground, are the types of "yinnish" astronaut requests we can expect to find from those aboard a space station in an even more emphatic way during the 1990s. Now is the time to realize this, before we freeze the space station into an antiseptic quasi-military, grey barracks yang dead-end. Yang overkill up there could invite yin overreaction later on.

The yin forces may soon create new ecological niches and lifestyles in space beyond the purview of the yang drawing boards. Crews may be multicultural, multidisciplinary, and finally equal between the sexes. Cooperation between the U.S., Soviets, and other nations could become commonplace with joint trips to Mars and beyond. The trips themselves, months to years long, would be passive and coasting, yin-like.

It seems, however, that the NASA bureaucracy, the military, and their obedient contractors are pursuing a path that is so yang that the viability of the entire American space program is now at risk. This is analogous to the yang overemphasis in Western science nowadays. In recent years, the collective culture has been drugged by an overtly yang paradigm that is choking itself off from its former vitality, in some sense literally drugged by crack, semi-automatic weapons, and TV. But we also need to know that these are outer symptoms of the inner reality of the individuals involved. Many of those in the space business are individually and collectively estranged from their life force. They wait in the wings for the day that the inner and outer yin and yang come into balance. Then we can pursue our most heartfelt dreams like an international mission to Mars.

One of my personal challenges in recent years has been to transform my own yang aspect. In rejecting further participation in the great American space adventure, I have disowned a legitimately large part of myself, one that wants to continue to implement the "right stuff, can-do" attitude of the Apollo and planetary programs. I have instead emphasized pursuing the more yin path of my inner space, while articulating goals for the outer that unfortunately seem to be beyond our reach.

Why did I reject practical participation in the outer? Was it more than the fact that the space program has withered in recent years? Or did I set all this up myself? Under new "reality" principles, I created my own reality by changing my personal focus from exploring outer space to exploring inner space. Otherwise I would still be on NASA's space team, either as a shuttle astronaut or as a planetary scientist, making the best of a difficult situation, still feeling a sense of comfort and continuity in my first chosen profession, but yearning for something more and not knowing what it was.

Conclusion

In this chapter, I have tried to make a number of points. First, the astronauts and cosmonauts have bequeathed an awareness of a planetary consciousness based on a motivation to explore inner and outer space and to address our sense of wonder and awe with experience. Space exploration is the "central project" of our time to unify humanity and open the planet to the new reality. The wide variety of astronaut experiences also testifies to the importance of the individual in shaping his experience: our inner space does profoundly shape our outer space, adding an important element to the new reality.

Secondly, we see in outer space some powerful metaphors for understanding our inner space and vice versa. For example, like the planets, we humans radiate light we cannot see and therefore presume it is not there. Yet it *is* there and can be measured by our feelings and by experiments that will be described in later chapters.

Third, we are witnessing in our Western culture, especially in military, space and scientific activities, a profound lack of spirit and mystery that we once felt. I attribute our troubled times to an overemphasis on the yang, or the masculine-aggressive aspect, of the yin-yang duality. I believe we will redress that once people begin to inhabit space over long periods of time. Then the space program will truly thrive. The days of $16 billion locker-room space stations may be over as public support of a tired, old yang NASA bureaucracy dwindles.

I believe something new will be born when we put the yin into space. The results will seem shocking to yang-obsessed forces who, to their credit, were the ones who made all this rocketry and adventure possible in the first place. For the United States to have a viable and lasting space program, the yang people must allow themselves to be joined by their yin colleagues.

In the end, we will need to integrate the dualities of space, science, and society into the greater reality. The *Challenger* disaster, NASA's lack of leadership, the destructive powers of modern military machines, bureaucratic cover-ups, the pollution of the planet, our aggressive pursuit of money, the obstinacy of a rational scientific community—all juxtaposed to the passive mysticism of the Far East—serve to teach us how much we need to integrate the planetary yin and yang into global harmony, cooperation, and compassion.

Understanding the physical universe and exploring it are wonderful ways of working with outer space to become self-aware in inner space. We are on the threshold of physically moving out beyond the Earth. It's also sobering to think that we could also destroy ourselves and the planet—the entirety of history and biology.

I envision, within a human generation, some of the more adventuresome among us permanently climbing the physical evolutionary ladder to new niches beyond the planet. I also envision space passenger service, hotels, and colonies for millions. Before long, the first child will be conceived and born in space free of the Earth's gravity well. These are facts.

What we don't know for sure is how, based on information described in the next chapters, future UFO and Mars events will unfold. If revelations are soon forthcoming, they will boggle our linear minds even more than the more certain prospects of space travel just described. We are on the threshold of being able to move ourselves into a cosmic awareness. We don't know how or when this will happen or what will come first. We can be fairly certain our discoveries will be more breathtaking than we ever imagined at the dawn of the space age.

It is exciting to be living at a time when outer space, and inner space are becoming more obviously related. It is also exciting to rediscover the awe I felt when I looked through the telescope as a child. The power that lies in integrating that child with the adult inquisitive mind also knows there is much more out there than meets the eye. What joy there is when we're able to experience life more and more as we grow into a state of greater awareness of who we really are!

In the purity of my childhood I turned upward in my quest for a vision. I have become aware that turning upward is merely one way of turning inward. Many of us have a desire to get off, transcend the planet because we need to explore. But what we need to explore is who we are.

Bibliography

Campbell, Joseph, interviewed by Eugene Kennedy, "Earthrise: The Dawning of a New Spiritual Awareness," *The New York Times Magazine*, April 15, 1979, pp 14-15.

Campbell, Joseph, *The Inner Reaches of Outer Space*, Alfred Vander Marck Enterprises, New York (1986).

Fuller, R. Buckminster, *Critical Path*, St. Martin's Press, New York (1981).

Harman, Willis and Howard Rheingold, *Higher Creativity: Liberating the Unconscious for Breakthrough Insights*, J.P. Tarcher, Los Angeles (1984).

O'Leary, Brian, *The Fertile Stars*, Everest House, New York (1981).

O'Leary, Brian, "Inner Space Outer Space," *The Movement*, Los Angeles, October 1984.

O'Leary, Brian, "The Threshold on Inner-Outer Space," *The Movement*, December 1984.

O'Leary, Brian, "Duality, Oneness and Outer Space," *The Movement*, March 1985.

O'Leary, Brian, "Reflected and Radiated Light," *The Movement*, May 1985.

O'Leary, Brian, "Yin and Yang in Space," *The Movement*, October 1985 and *L-5 News*, July 1986.

O'Leary, Brian, *Mars 1999*, Stackpole Books, Harrisburg, PA (1987).

O'Neill, Gerard K., *The High Frontier*, Morrow, New York (1977).

Schweickart, Russell L., *No Frames, No Boundaries*, film commentary, Creative Initiative/Beyond War, Palo Alto, CA. From *Earth's Answer: Exploration of Planetary Culture at the Lindesfarne Conferences*, Lindesfarne/Harper & Row, W. Stockbridge, MA (1977).

White, Frank, *The Overview Effect*, Houghton Mifflin, Boston (1987).

5

MARS AND THE SEARCH FOR EXTRATERRESTRIAL LIFE

> If a human face is there on Mars, it blows just about every orthodoxy wide open . . . (The Face) is not a cure to all our ills, but it is a signed, sealed, and delivered paradigm shift, out of which a real human transformation may come.
>
> —Richard Grossinger in *The Monuments of Mars*

As a professional space scientist, one of the most provocative questions I have addressed is, are we alone in the universe? Man has always been curious about his place in the cosmos, but only within the past century have we had the technology and science to begin to seriously undertake a search for an answer. The scientific rationale is compelling: of the trillions of stars like our sun, a significant percentage are likely to have Earth-like planets orbiting them. Many reputable scientists have speculated that some of these might be inhabited by intelligent beings.

Over the past decade, American astronomers have been able to obtain funds from the government to use radio telescopes to listen to possible signals coming from intelligent technological civilizations on planets circling nearby stars. The program is called SETI, the Search for Extraterrestrial Intelligence, an acronym similar to the name of the star Tau Ceti, one of the early candidates for the search.

A number of choices and variables make the search one of the most speculative activities contemporary Western scientists have dared to try. A successful detection requires choosing the right radio frequency, picking the right target, integrating the signal for a long enough period of time for detection, distinguishing what is intelligent from what is natural, and then—no small task—cracking the code.

Even with a successful detection we could hardly have a meaningful dialogue. The nearest star to us besides the sun is Alpha Centauri, 4.3 light years away (one light year is the distance over which light and radio waves travel in one year). The speed of light is 186,000 miles per second. So a light year is a distance too great to comprehend in ordinary terms. By comparison the Moon is a little more than 1 light second away, the Sun, Mars, Venus and Mercury are light minutes distance and the stars and galaxies are up to billions of light years away. Most SETI target stars are greater than 10 light years away from us. This means that our attempts to beam back a radio signal to answer a successful detection would not be acknowledged and returned again to us for decades at the very least. My former Cornell colleague Carl Sagan lamented this problem in his recent novel *Contact*.

It is remarkable that SETI has been funded at all in an environment not conducive to this sort of low-yield activity. Perhaps one justification is that the program began during the 1960s with a low budget use of existing radio telescopes (Project Ozma) temporarily diverted from "real science" projects. Former Senator William Proxmire one year gave SETI the Golden Fleece Award, a notorious distinction conferred upon those federally funded research projects that appeared to Proxmire to be frivolous uses of tax money.

But as we shall see, the support of SETI by the federal government and the scientific community, but their lack of support for less traditional searches, does not make much sense to the informed observer. Of the less traditional searches, UFO reports and the processing of images of anomalous features on Mars appear to be much more high-yield, yet are looked upon with disdain by mainstream scientists.

"Men of science," wrote the respected French UFO researcher Jacques Vallee, "react to UFO reports in a very peculiar fashion. They go so far as neglecting to conform with the basic rules of scientific honesty when confronted with this problem, and they allow themselves to act as they never would in the presence of a more 'classical' mystery. On the contrary, anxiety has been released on perfectly innocuous programs sponsored by professional astronomers, in which one would record the radio signals coming from nearby stars and look for possible shifts of pulses or "messages" of intelligent origin (Project Ozma). All this points to one conclusion: The scientists' reaction to the problems has never been anything but emotional. In this line of thinking, it is justifiable to assume that other civilizations are sending radio signals through space because radio waves are a good vehicle of information and because space travel between planetary systems is inconceivable. Both assumptions are extrapolations of conditions existing on Earth today. They neglect entirely the fact that our idea of space travel as well as our idea of information exchange are very closely related to present physical conception."

I agree with Vallee's assessment. My astronomer colleagues have begun an exotic search, but it may have distracted many of us from going to where the real action is. That action may require us to let go of preconceived ideas about how extraterrestrial intelligence may manifest. I am one of those scientists who, until recently, refused to look at alternative search paradigms. At first they seemed weird and nonscientific to me, even though Michael Papagiannis and other astronomers have argued that solar system artifacts, perhaps in the asteroid belt, are plausible targets of search, and even though astronomer J. Allen Hynek asserted that some UFO reports are *absolutely real.* It now seems obvious to me that UFO research and the examination of anomalous features on Mars will almost certainly yield more interesting immediate results than the SETI radio telescopic search. Yet it took me awhile to adopt that point of view. Scientific peer pressure can be a powerful barrier.

Let me venture an analogy which I must admit involves making an assumption—that our first encounters with extraterrestrial intelligence will involve beings of greater technological capability than our own. Within known history, we humans have only within the past century been able to travel in the air, send and receive radio signals, venture into space, and develop weapons of massive destruction. To presume others will meet us at our current technological level, a mere hairline in history, and from a safe distance of light years, is presuming a lot.

On the other hand, if we are encountered in untraditional, noncontemporary ways, involving the broader paradigms of the new reality, we can expect only the unexpected. We must be prepared to confront the wonder of extraterrestrial intelligence anticipating phenomena more akin to what we would classify as paranormal.

Let us presume we belong to a primitive tribe on the Earth, unaware of twentieth century technology. Some of us experience the sighting of an aircraft or encounter a modern artifact. Perhaps we are bushmen who behold a Coke bottle, or aborigines who observe a "big silver bird" in the sky that issues a thunderous noise. What are we to make of these encounters? The truth is we don't have the language or science to apply to the phenomena. We don't know what is happening except that some of us were witnesses to something strange.

In such a case, we might make myths about, or worship, the object or events. To the degree we are scientifically trained, we can just observe and correlate information between objects and observations. Ironically, in contemporary science, more often than not, we choose to deny the phenomena, ignore the data, and flock toward what might be more orthodox. We focus exclusively on a radio telescope search. As members of the tribe we might discard the observations of the airplanes, discard the Coke bottle, and conjure myths about how hypothetical alien beings might conduct themselves in a context that involves communicating with tribal members in tribal language dealing with provincial tribal issues.

I hate to admit that many of our best and brightest scientists seem to have perspectives as anthropomorphic as the ancients who believed that the Earth was at the center of the universe. This self-absorption is blocking orderly research into a number of unexplained observations and phenomena.

I admit all this because, until recently, I myself *was* one of those scientists who, in most respects, I now regard as having tunnel-visioned views. True, I had published articles in the literature that many scientists would not have dared submit. I would sometimes address subjects on the very fringes of acceptability and struggle to move the papers through layers of skeptical reviews until they finally saw the light of day. (For example, it took me two years to publish a basic physics paper in *Science* on the accessibility of Earth-approaching asteroids for mining expeditions.) The negative reviews did not address the science, but instead assailed the inappropriateness of the subject of inquiry, a subject that did not fall within traditional categories. The negative reviews are also targeted toward some rapidly unfolding unorthodox inquiries many of us are involved in regarding a close-by planet.

Mars

No physical destination has enchanted me more than the planet Mars. As a boy I wondered what it would be like to go there, and I avidly read Wernher von Braun's visions of a Mars trip. Both my Masters and Doctorate theses were on simulating properties of Mars in the laboratory. I was appointed to the U.S. astronaut program to go to Mars at a time NASA was actively considering it. Most of my professional research, teaching, and popular writing have been about this most Earthlike of the planets in our Solar System.

I have frequently addressed the question whether there may be, or may have been, life on Mars, finding myself on both sides of the issue depending on the company and the search technique. The debate has *always* been emotionally charged.

It was not until 1965 that our eyes opened to what Mars really looked like. Previously, as seen through a telescope, it was a fuzzy red disk with almost indistinct markings and polar caps. The U.S. Mariner 4 spacecraft flew by the planet photographing one percent of its surface. What scientists saw was a disappointing array of craters, suggesting an ancient and unmodified terrain like the Moon's. They concluded that we were dealing with a dull dead planet.

But in 1971 we were in for a few surprises. The Mariner 9 Mars orbiter took some spectacular pictures of a volcano three times higher than Mt. Everest, a grand canyon three times deeper than ours, and 2500 miles long, dried-up river beds showing that liquid water once flowed, that it had once rained onto the Martian surface.

In 1976, U.S. Viking robots landed at the two sites on Mars. The life detection apparatus showed no signs of life, although some of the results showed an unexpected chemistry. While many scientists are convinced we will not find life anywhere, others have speculated we might find it elsewhere on the planet. It is also possible that the Viking experiments were not definitive enough to detect life because we do not really know what we are looking for.

Another farther-out sounding hypothesis is that intelligent

life may have once been there and left behind artifacts of its existence. As I stated a few pages back, astronomer Michael Papagiannis and others believe that such calling cards may have been left in our solar system. But this possibility seemed so far fetched to the Viking scientists that they may have ignored some of the most intriguing evidence we have ever collected in the search for extraterrestrial intelligence: pictures of objects on the surface of Mars that resemble a gigantic human face and nearby pyramids.

I myself had ignored these pictures until the summer of 1984 when an enthusiastic science writer, Richard Hoagland, asked me to sit down with him and look at newer versions of the controversial Viking pictures of Mars. This was at The Case for Mars II conference in Boulder, Colorado, where a collection of scientists and engineers were promoting the further exploration of the Red Planet. I was using all the scientific clout I had to propose an unconventional international manned mission to Phobos and Deimos, the moons of Mars, because of their resources and strategic locations. To go any further would be to really lose the support of my peers.

Hoagland believed that some of the pictures contained evidence of monuments left by some past civilization on Mars. At the time, I listened but didn't believe him. The truth was, *I didn't want to believe him.* I had too much professionally at stake already selling an unorthodox Mars mission concept. I was still in the mainstream!

While Hoagland spoke, I involuntarily recalled the long, sordid history of exaggerated claims about life on Mars. I had even myself participated in research debunking the most relevant piece of evidence for life on Mars during the 1960s. Working with my Ph.D. thesis advisor at Berkeley, Donald Rea, I showed that infrared observations of the surface of Mars that had suggested the presence of organic materials were really only showing water vapor in the Earth's atmosphere above the telescope!

I was aware of Percival Lowell's interpretation early this century that canals on Mars that he thought he observed were irrigation ditches used by an intelligent civilization to bring scarce water from melting polar caps to lower latitudes. These observations later were found to be physio-psychological illusions.

So I saw the making of another possible Mars myth. What's

more, Hoagland was not even a trained scientist. And the pictures had been taken by the U.S. Viking Mars orbiter way back in 1976. My scientist colleagues on the television science team had already deemed the objects that Hoagland found to be so interesting as only a "trick of lighting and shadow." The members of the team were my peers, people with whom I had worked closely and had trusted for their discipline and objectivity. So what was the use of turning up an old stone and challenging their evaluation?

Hoagland showed me two views of a mile-wide mesa that resembled a human face. He showed some nearby mountains that resembled pyramids. He pointed out possible striking alignments of these objects. I was also vaguely aware that Vincent di Pietro and Gregory Molenaar, computer scientists outside the mainstream of the planetary community, had published a booklet about the face and pyramids using some image processing techniques to point out some striking features, such as an eyeball in the "eye." But because these investigations were on the fringes, I had taken only a casual interest in the matter. My colleagues on the Viking team would handle that one, I had thought.

So, why was I having an internal battle looking at the pictures? Why was Hoagland bringing up old stuff? Hadn't this already been looked at? On the one hand, the awestruck boy in me wanted to explore the unknown mysteries of Mars more than ever. On the other hand, the suspicious, trained scientist in me felt I was being handed another illusion, hoax, or overinterpretation.

Still, something inside of me prompted me to keep listening to Hoagland. Meeting him in 1984 began a four-year period of intensive investigation which revealed to me some exciting results together with the perils of presenting them within our current scientific paradigm. I visited Hoagland many times, conducted meetings with other researchers, and I was eventually elected president of the Mars Anomalies Research Society (M.A.R.S.), a nonprofit organization temporarily established to investigate the unusual Martian features. From all this, a number of scientific papers and books have been published and they have been the targets of almost absurdly uninformed ridicule from my mainstream colleagues.

Planetary geologist Michael Carr, the former head of the Viking Orbiter imaging science team, made several appearances on television declaring the face to be merely another windblown mesa. Pointing out another Martian feature that resembled television's Sesame Street puppet Kermit the Frog, Carr concluded that of the thousands of mesas viewed by the Viking camera, surely one might resemble a face, or anything else. Such a natural feature would be analogous to New Hampshire's Old Man of the Mountain, he said. One could see on Carr's face an expression of sarcasm, and their condescending chuckles and an attitude of disdain toward any investigation which he felt to be fruitless. Among other things, he ignored the fact that the Old Man of the Mountain is a mere profile, while the Martian artifact sustains its "faceness" at all angles of viewing.

I was soon to discover that Carr's views were echoed by virtually all my well-placed planetary science colleagues. Carl Sagan pointed to a likeness of Jesus Christ appearing on a tortilla chip. Lou Friedman, an old friend and executive director of Sagan's Planetary Society, almost threw me out of his office when I mentioned the face. "This nonsense is not worth one second of your time, Brian," he said. Hoagland's book is full of anecdotes on how mainstream scientists reacted to the prospects of an investigation into the anomalous Martian features. Clearly I had to find others outside the field with whom to collaborate.

I remain truly dismayed by the attitude of my former colleagues. Even if they do prove to be right—that the features in Cydonia are merely windblown mesas—we have a right to continue probing.

My conclusion from all my research has been that we don't know the origin of these features and that we must go back there and investigate further. Meanwhile, we can take the existing pictures and analyze their properties to shed more light on their characteristics, awaiting further verification from future space missions.

All this seemed innocent enough, but when we attempted publishing our results, we opened another Pandora's box. Dr. Mark Carlotto, a director of a research group at the image processing laboratory at The Analytical Sciences Corporation in Reading, Massachusetts, used the most current state-of-the-art equipment to further process the Viking data into clearer, more revealing pictures. Planetary scientists at NASA and elsewhere, with funding left over from the billion dollar Viking project, could as well have done the work, but their quick dismissal of these objects as unworthy of further investigation precluded for a decade any further work using the best available processing equipment then.

Not being a planetary scientist, Carlotto had little to lose in doing this research. Yet his qualifications to do the job were impeccable, given his background in image processing of terrestrial features, especially in military reconnaissance programs. Clearly we had a case in which we needed to bring in specialists from outside the field in order to get anything done. Planetary science, once a promising new field in which I was one of the first to receive a Ph.D., has already become an ingrown priesthood, whose leaders pontificate the views of an old framework of inquiry and discovery. The Viking geologists looked at Mars through geological-colored glasses, blinded to the reality that something extraordinary was staring them straight in the face.

Carlotto and I had done some analysis examining the three-dimensional structure of the face. The work involved well-known algorithms in optics and methods of cross-checking to validate the results. Our conclusion was that, to the degree of resolution available to us in the data, the three-dimensional structure of the face showed a striking degree of facelike features and bilateral (left-right) symmetry. The case for intelligent origin seemed far more impressive than that of the Old Man in the Mountain, a profile rendered by nature *in only one dimension*, and used by the skeptics as their "proof" that the face must be natural.

Still, we couldn't conclude anything about the "extraterrestrial-origin" hypothesis, though we could assert beyond any reasonable doubt that the face was not a trick of lighting and shadow, as proposed eleven years earlier by the Viking scientists.

Carlotto and I submitted scientific papers to Carl Sagan at *Icarus*, the International Journal of the Solar System—perhaps the best known and most prestigious of the planetary journals. *Icarus* had over the past twenty-five years published eleven of my peer-reviewed papers.

Our papers were turned down flatly by the editors, who offered little explanation for their action. I had never had a paper turned down by *Icarus*. On technical grounds, the reviewers' comments were easily addressed, in fact more easily than with most papers I have published.

"Unfortunately the manuscript by B. O'Leary is a non-paper," one reviewer wrote. ". . . no doubt the author will complain about the lack of 'specific criticisms' on my part . . . The author might do well to learn some basic rules of elementary logic . . . There is nothing in the author's background that renders him competent to infer from the general morphology of a surface feature what processes were involved . . . Come on! Let's stop this nonsense."

Both reviewers maintained that the Old Man of the Mountain is natural and therefore there is no reason why the face wouldn't also be natural. But what is the probability of a natural mesa being so facelike in all *three* dimensions? Very low, I surmised. I know of no such feature on Earth.

Something else was happening. My colleagues did not want to believe there was anything to the face, either because they truly didn't believe it, or because they had a vested interest not to do so. For example, they might worry that their funding would be cut off if inquiry were made into something as seemingly preposterous as a face on Mars.

Carlotto resubmitted his paper to *Applied Optics*, where it was published nearly a year and a half after the original *Icarus* try. The face on Mars appeared on the cover of the May 15, 1988 issue of that prestigious journal with the innocuous title "Remote Sensing." (Focusing on imaging techniques, rather than on such a bizarre subject, made the face more legitimate to optical scientists.) *Applied Optics* was far enough removed from the planetary fraternity to make the paper acceptable to those scientists editing and reviewing it. I resubmitted my paper to the *Journal of the British Interplanetary Society*, where Carlotto and others have also sent in newer papers.

The results caused quite a stir in the press. Hoagland, Carlotto, anthropologist Randy Pozos and I held a well-attended press conference in July 1988. In it, I was asked if I felt there was extraterrestrial intelligence and when we might expect to make this discovery. I replied jokingly that I was being put on the spot, but I would take a stab at it. "I have a strong feeling," I said, "that within ten years we are going to discover extraterrestrial intelligence."

Carla Hall of the *Washington Post* (July 8, 1988) jumped on this quote, referring to me as having "tottered a little closer to the edge" than the other press conference participants by my enthusiastically proclaiming this. She wrote that the assembled reporters responded to me by bellowing "'Oooo-wooo-oo' and some chuckles." The *Post* did not quote any of my main remarks referring to the importance of returning to Mars to further study the face and other features.

In the same *Post* article, Carl Sagan was quoted as saying: "It's probably something perfectly natural which by accident looks like a face. . . . There's a wonderful happy face in the middle of a crater (on Mars)—from which I do not deduce that there are people who live on Mars who make happy-face buttons." Needless to say, Sagan ignored the actual data.

This press conference taught me the perils of engaging in battle with the press and my peers. Clearly Sagan and company did not want to believe there might be something to this, and I needed to be careful with my words so as not to be associated with a lunatic fringe. The press and publicity-conscious scientists like Sagan were parroting the old paradigm by making pronouncements on the natural origin of the face and chuckling about the extraterrestrial intelligence hypothesis without even having checked out the pertinent information.

As sad as I was to leave the planetary science priesthood, I also felt a new freedom. I was no longer reliant on NASA and my peers for having bread on the table or for approving my work. By mid-1988 I had established myself as a freelance lecturer and writer. At last I was free to express myself, although still cautiously, so that my exploration of the newer paradigms of science could be ushered in with integrity rather than with the extremes of denial or wishful, premature thinking.

Still I had to be careful. I wish I had not been so strong with the press. I *do*, however, feel deeply that we are on the threshold of discovery. But it is only a feeling, not a scientific fact.

Undaunted by peers and press, Carlotto continued his research and submitted a second paper to *Nature*, another prestigious journal. The emphasis this time was on what scientists call "fractals" or the degree of self-similarity of a landscape. This rather complex algorithm in image-processing allows one to determine the tendency of a landscape to look the same at a range of scales or resolutions. A self-similar or fractal terrain is almost always found in nature. A non-fractal terrain normally marks a feature which is formed by intelligence. Scientists use fractals in military space and aerial reconnaissance to discern tanks, equipment, and buildings partly camouflaged by trees and terrain.

Carlotto found that the face and some other features on Mars are not fractal, suggesting that they are not natural. The face itself was the *least natural* of the many Martian landforms analyzed.

Nature turned down the paper for reasons similar to *Icarus*'. I reviewed the paper and concluded that *Nature*'s objections had nothing to do with the technical validity of the paper. It was obviously an aversion by the scientific establishment to the fact that this was too hot for them to handle. The paper will probably find a home in the *Journal of the British Interplanetary Society*.

Other investigators have also entered the research effort. Geographer Erol Torun has looked at the angles formed by the facets of the two-mile long "D & M pyramid," a five-sided pyramid-shaped object lying a few miles to the southwest of the face (D & M stands for DiPietro and Molenaar, who discovered the pyramid during their search of Viking pictures). What Torun found was the surprising result that the ratios between the five principal angles at the pyramid apex "express the universal mathematical constants of the square roots of 2, 3, 5, 6, e, and pi. . . . These constants should be known by any civilization possessing Egyptian level technology (or greater). . . . The constants themselves are universal because they exist regardless of the number base being used . . ." Regarding the other angles, Torun continued to find mathematically significant numbers "no matter how I looked at the object."

Torun concluded that, within a small error of measurement, this geometry probably could not have been natural; it is simply too elegant. He also felt wind erosion could not have shaped the object without destroying its five sides. All this is highly suggestive that intelligence was behind the creation of the pyramid. I have reviewed the work and find it intriguing although not unequivocal.

Meanwhile the energetic and outspoken Hoagland is drawing up geometric relations among the main features in the Cydonia region of Mars that also appear to reflect a sort of sacred geometry. His challenge is formidable because of the many angles and points involved in the analysis.

Clearly we have something of scientific value. I am sad to see my planetary science colleagues ridiculing such a promising inquiry. They are intelligent people with considerable clout with NASA and adequate funding to do the work.

Yet I can also see the human element operating here. Any unconventional approach to the search for extraterrestrial intelligence will likely fall on deaf scientific and governmental ears. Certainly one reason for this is the threat this sort of inquiry poses to careers. It took a lot for me to decompress from scientific orthodoxy, a process that began more than ten years ago. I am only now letting go, and I am still only testing my wings.

A second, more ominous possible reason for the blackout on scientific inquiry is a conspiracy. By threatening to withhold research funds, the government may be discouraging inquiry. Among my planetary science colleagues, I have been witness to more than one sudden turnabout from enthusiasm to brushoff on the Mars face research. Hoagland documents similar encounters in his book.

In these two respects, the Mars investigation resembles the UFO research, to be discussed in the next chapter. But far from dealing with a plethora of bizarre and spontaneous UFO events, with the Mars project we have pinned down on magnetic tape a number of objects which already have been shown to be of great interest. They will be there when we come back, unlike the elusive UFO. Because of the efforts of outsiders like Hoagland, Carlotto, and Torun, NASA has tentatively agreed to look at the anomalous features of Cydonia with its far superior camera aboard the 1992 Observer spacecraft.

During a 1988 visit to the Soviet Union, I urged planetary scientists to point the 1989 Phobos probe camera toward Cydonia. Whether they were able to find the right observing conditions, given the spacecraft's orbit before its untimely loss of contact with Earth, we do not know, but we shall shortly.

Meanwhile, the Red Planet continues to hold a mystique for mankind. It appears to "cry out for exploration" in Carl Sagan's words, although many of us have reasons for going back there that may not match Sagan's. I think we are possibly on the threshold of a great discovery. Sagan and the planetary geologists talk of possible fossils in the Martian dried-up river beds, a more traditional rationale for further exploration.

Hoagland and company are going after bigger stakes: was

an intelligent civilization once on Mars? If so, its manifestation of a humanoid face is ironic to those who have criticized the SETI project as being too anthropomorphic. What could be more anthropomorphic than an enormous human face staring us in the face? The hypothetical Martians appear to be telling us that the truth is stranger and more surprising then the plausible fictions conjured up by the SETI scientists.

Fortunately, we should soon have an answer to the likely origin of the mysterious features of Cydonia. Mars Observer will hopefully obtain higher resolution pictures in 1992. And a worldwide movement toward an international human mission to Mars near the turn of the century will enable us to gather the necessary "ground truth" about what happened on Mars some millions of years ago to create such bizarre landforms. Such a mission in the spirit of world peace would be a crowning achievement for mankind, regardless of the results.

As for the face itself, I have some hunches. Research has shown that its three-dimensional facelike quality is striking as is its bilateral (left-right) symmetry and non-fractal nature. Nearby features also appear to be unique and artificial. These qualities transcend Sagan's glib remarks about finding faces everywhere. But the symmetry is not perfect, suggesting—if we adopt the hypothesis that the face was constructed by intelligence—that we are seeing some subsequent erosion or incomplete construction.

The fact that the face appears humanoid strikes a curious resonant chord within us and is consistent with UFO encounter reports. If the face is the product of a civilization, why is it humanoid? Is this a ubiquitous form to be found in the universe? In an interview with Richard Hoagland, Richard Grossinger suggests in *Planetary Mysteries* that "an archetypal force may be at work in the universe, a force that's quite out of fashion. If humanoids also evolved elsewhere, then there must be some basic humanoid structure in nature. The force need not suggest only the psychologically archetypal, as with (Carl) Jung; in fact, it is far closer to something biologically or astrophysically archetypal, going right into the heart of the creative process of the universe itself. It suggests a possible translation from basic atomic morphology to biomorphology to psychomorphology, a route that is the earmark of a whole vitalistic science the abandonment of which is one of the axioms of this century.

"So to have a humanoid, and a humanoid on the very next planet over from Earth, suggests one of two things, both of them very disturbing to progressive liberal scientific mentalities. You are suggesting either that there is an intrinsic "humanoidizing" force in the universe (which goes against the atheistic basis of science itself), or that humanoids have come from elsewhere and been associated with this planet, this solar System. If it's the former, then you are very close to spiritualizing the universe. If it's the latter then you are giving aid and comfort to the whole ancient-astronaut fringe which is so distasteful to modern astronomers. There is also a hint here of Francis Crick's theory (that panspermia was directed toward Earth from space) that we ourselves, because of the particular chemistry of our molecules, are more like the offspring of outer-space people than indigenous evolved creatures on Earth."

One of the largest lessons of our time is that anything is possible. The unexpected waits on our doorstep and we need to have open enough minds to assimilate a much larger body of data that initially confounds us. If necessary, we will need to sidestep the priesthood of Western science to go after the information that is required if we are to transform our world.

Bibliography

Carlotto, Mark J., "Digital image analysis of unusual Martian surface features," *Applied Optics*, Vol. 27, pp 1926-1933 (1988).

Carlotto, Mark J. and Michael C. Stein, "A search for artificial objects on planetary surfaces," submitted to the *Journal of the British Interplanetary Society* (1989).

DiPietro, Vincent and Gregory Molenaar, *Unusual Martian Surface Features*, Mars Research, Glenn Dale, Maryland (1982).

Grossinger, Richard (edit.), *Planetary Mysteries*, p. 27, North Atlantic Books, Berkeley, Calf. (1986).

Hall, Carla, "Eyes on Mr. Mars," *The Washington Post*, July 8, 1988, p. B1.

Hoagland, Richard C., *The Monuments of Mars*, North Atlantic Books, Berkeley, CA (1987). Comments from Richard Grossinger's foreword to this book are quoted.

O'Leary, Brian, "Analysis of the Images of the 'Face' on Mars and Possible Intelligent Origin," submitted to the *Journal of the British Interplanetary Society* (1989).

Papagiannis, Michael, "The importance of exploring the asteroid belt," *Acta Astronautica*, Vol. 10, pp 709-712 (1981); also *Strategies for the Search for Life in the Universe*, D. Reidel Publishing, Dordrecht, Holland (1985), and "The search for extraterrestrial life: recent developments. A report on IAU symposium 112," *Journal of the British Interplanetary Society*, vol. 38, pp 281-285 (1980).

Pozos, Randolfo, *The Face on Mars: Evidence for a Lost Civilization?*, North Atlantic Books, Berkeley, CA (1986).

Torun, Erol O., "Preliminary investigation of the geometry of the D & M pyramid," submitted to the *Journal of the British Interplanetary Society* (1989).

Vallee, Jacques, *UFOs in Space*, Ballentine Books, New York, p. 121 (1965).

6

UFOs, EXTRATERRESTRIALS AND OTHER DIMENSIONS

> Exactly why forty years of impressive human testimony and related instrumental and physical evidence has essentially escaped the attention of science constitutes a human mystery of major proportions.
>
> —Richard Hall, *Uninvited Guests*

> UFO research is leading us kicking and screaming into the science of the twenty-first century.
>
> —J. Allen Hynek

If most of us in the scientific community choose to continue to ignore the new reality, current trends show that it will not ignore us. We recall that the main features of this greater reality are that all of science is "patent pending," that the observer interacts with the observed, and that our inner space deeply influences our outer space. Regarding the old scientific models, one is reminded of the act of rearranging the deck chairs of the *Titanic* while it is sinking, or of steadfastly claiming the world is flat when overwhelming evidence exists to the contrary.

No example of the new reality impinging on us rings clearer than that of unidentified flying objects. The UFO phenomenon includes eyewitness accounts of observations of apparently physical vehicles and encounters with their humanoid occupants. Most often, witnesses see disc-shaped craft of varying sizes that can maneuver with ease, mostly vertically, and suddenly at sharp angles in apparent violation of Newton's Laws. They are sometimes detected by radar, can radiate light of many colors, rapidly appear and disappear, and produce visible marks on the ground.

The term "unidentified flying object" does not do the subject justice. Animals are affected, people can be paralyzed, blinded, burned, get headaches, become nauseous, etc. UFOs also appear to interfere with radios, television sets, automobile electrical systems and power lines. In many cases, humanoid creatures (pilots?) are encountered who usually run away when noticed. People have often reported "missing time," later to recall experiences of having been abducted and placed on board a craft. Physical exams, telepathic discussions, and even sexual encounters have been reported.

It is remarkable that I have ignored UFO data for so many years, given the hundreds of times I've been asked questions about this following speeches I have given. I usually danced around the subject, assuming that to address it would have imperiled my professional standing with my scientific peers. Only recently have I embraced the extraordinary significance of the UFO phenomenon to the past, present, and future of mankind.

To be saying that there is validity to the UFO phenomena still seems like heresy to me, so deep and classic is my indoctrination. It shakes my very foundations as a trained Western scientist. And yet, any intelligent investigator who takes the time to examine the evidence will come to the conclusion that the phenomenon is *real*, at least to those who have experienced it. We are beyond the point of excusing denial; the question now is: what is going on? Because of the large quantities of data collected and the enormous philosophical implications of positive results, focus on UFOs and extraterrestrial intelligence should become one of the primary scientific inquiries of our time.

For those of you who are skeptical about the reality of the UFO phenomenon, I ask you to try and suspend your disbelief as you proceed. No subject has been more misunderstood, exaggerated, and miscommunicated than UFO encounters. They are the stuff of tabloids and Hollywood fantasies, giving the scientific reality of the phenomenon a low credibility. Here we need to be careful in discriminating the evidence and preserving the mysterious baby while throwing out the sensationalist bath water.

In this chapter, then, I wish to present a brief summary of the available evidence and to list the books written by outstanding investigators in the field of UFO research. A one-chapter summary does not do the subject justice, though. Because the implications of UFO encounters are so mind-wrenching, no intellectual presentation at all can adequately embrace their essence. As is the case with other aspects of the new reality, there is no substitute for experience, and experience may be terrifying and denied.

My Own UFO Experience

In May 1987 a friend and I were Whitley and Anne Strieber's guests at their upstate New York cottage. Strieber is the author of the recent bestseller *Communion* and its sequel *Transformation*, books that depict his extraordinary encounters with alleged alien beings. He describes how these beings carried him away against his conscious will and put him through some of the most bizarre experiences and emotional transformations one could imagine—amnesia, lost time, telepathic communication, dreamlike encounters, cosmic insights, paralysis, physical exams and induced paranormal perceptions.

The Striebers' cottage was the site of most of his experiences with the alleged alien "visitors." Several of their house guests have also either witnessed or participated in these experiences. Strieber's credentials as a writer are well-established. Many batteries of psychological tests, hypnosis sessions, and lie detector tests affirm (to the degree they can do so) the accuracy of his perceptions. Were it not for thousands of other similar known cases, it still might not have been easy to accept the veracity of Strieber's report.

We arrived at the Striebers one beautiful spring afternoon. At about midnight we settled into bed. My friend and I were in the guest room downstairs. Having said goodnight to each other, she and I independently had the following experiences, which we were to share that next morning: First we each did a meditation and prayer which asked for protection and for no abductions that evening. In retrospect, we were both fearful of exposing ourselves to the full gamut of the consequences of being abducted.

Within minutes of the time our meditations began, we each felt a curious lethargy and paralysis. In fact, we both recalled having experienced the same overwhelming sense of well being, of euphoria while being motionless on our backs. We were being drugged without the use of an inducing substance. Neither of us had had any drugs or alcohol for weeks. Neither of us had had an experience like this before or since except perhaps under anesthesia.

To stay awake I started to recite my meditation aloud, but

my words trailed off to oblivion. I couldn't move. My friend's recognition of my lack of ability to finish a sentence added to her fear and she accelerated her meditation. All these efforts were to no avail.

I remember nothing about that night after falling asleep. I do remember having a very deep sleep and waking up in the same position I went to sleep in. My friend recalls having awakened four times during the night when she felt she couldn't move and saw bright lights on in the room. Yet we had turned out the lights before going to sleep and the lights were out when we woke up in the morning. The Striebers were not the kind of people who would have turned on the lights in the room as a sort of practical joke. They were sleeping upstairs quietly and soundly. Who turned on the lights? Who drugged us? These questions remain unanswered. But the experience was very real to each of us. Next morning, Whitley recalled a presence of the visitors in the house but not in the usual physical sense. He was not surprised at our experience, as we were later to learn such an experience was a common aspect of UFO phenomena.

Were we abducted but did not recall the experience because we had been drugged? Did they perform tests on us? Or, did they merely indicate a non-physical presence by manipulating physical realties such as our bodies and the lights in the room? Or were these only the products of two fertile imaginations, the result of the power of suggestion, being at Strieber's home and having read his book?

I don't know. What I do know was that something happened to us and, as a scientist, I owed it to myself to find out more. In the nearly two years since my visit to the Striebers, I have investigated UFO reports and interviewed the most reputable researchers in the field. Through their experiences, an ever increasing number of people are telling us we are on a collision course with a destiny far beyond our conscious minds. My conclusion is that we cannot ignore the phenomenon any more than we can ignore the physical reality of an impending auto accident. Through the UFO phenomenon, the greater reality is being gradually but inexorably forced upon us.

A Brief History of UFOs

The most recent series of UFO phenomena began in 1947, coincidentally or not just two years after the first detonation of an atomic bomb near Alamagordo, New Mexico. On June 24 private pilot Kenneth Arnold, flying over the Cascade Mountains of Washington State, spotted a formation of rapidly banking objects that issued blue-white flashes while traveling at a speed he measured to be over 1600 miles per hour—well beyond the technology of the day.

Just one week later, on July 2nd, Mac Brazel, a sheep rancher near Roswell, New Mexico apparently heard a tremendous explosion. The next morning to his astonishment, according to the story, he discovered a crashed disc-shaped object and he immediately called Roswell Army Air Field. The object evidently was captured and moved to CIA Headquarters in Langley, Virginia. Exotic metals were allegedly found in the debris. The base's public information officer even released a bulletin about the "recovered flying disc" before the military classified the incident. A number of later reports have alleged that humanoid beings were in the craft, some dead and at least one alive.

These events were apparently the beginning of what was to become a massive government cover-up. The mystery surrounding these events is documented in Charles Berlitz's and William Moore's book, *The Roswell Incident.* Decades later, eyewitnesses have come forth and government documents have been released that seem to further support the actuality of the UFO.

The varieties of reliable UFO reports coming from pilots, astronauts, military personnel, and intelligent laymen are too many to mention in detail here. My intent is not to convince you in favor of the existence of UFOs, but rather to allude to the volumes of such reports that have been amassed over the years. I will, however, mention the findings of some of those researchers of highest repute, many of whom have spent their productive professional years on UFO investigation, and I will speculate on what we might make of this research.

Perhaps the most highly regarded UFO researcher was the late astronomer J. Allen Hynek. As the waves of reported sightings and encounters began to flood the desks of military personnel during the latter 1940s, the Pentagon hired Hynek to sift through reports, to interview witnesses, and to advise them. Hynek was a skeptic, determined to prove that UFO phenomena could be explained either by natural phenomena (meteors, Venus, clouds, auroras, halos, etc.), fertile imaginations, or out-and-out hoaxes.

He proved himself wrong. He found hundreds of reports that violated these criteria. "I cannot presume to describe," he wrote, "what UFOs *are* because I don't know: I can establish beyond reasonable doubt that they are not all misperceptions or hoaxes."

"These people (the witnesses) are not merely names in a telephone book; they're flesh and blood persons who, as far as they are concerned, have had experiences as real to them as seeing a car come down the street is to others." Many of the witnesses have been scientifically trained.

"In my years of experience," he continued, "in the interrogation of UFO reporters one fact stands out: invariably I have had the feeling that I was talking to someone who was describing a very *real event*."

Not long before his death, in an interview with *Omni* magazine, Hynek said: "The question about whether you do or don't believe in UFOs is irrelevant. . . . The real question is whether or not the UFO phenomenon can be explained by the present scientific paradigm. I've come to believe that the answer is no." He then describes various paranormal physical events ranging from craft stopping cars to the UFOs' tremendous speeds, accelerations and direction changes.

Once he got involved, Hynek discovered that many of his interactions with his military and scientific colleagues were stressful and abrasive. "In my association with the UFO phenomenon," he said, "I was somewhat like the innocent bystander who got shot." Most of his colleagues, my old astronaut-astronomer self included, were the assailants.

For example, the June 1987 issue of *Sky & Telescope* (a magazine where I was once an editor), concluded, "Unidentified flying objects have faded from popularity in recent years, perhaps as the news media become more aware how little is behind every UFO tale that has ever been well investigated."

Hynek gave one almost humorous example of a meeting of several hundred professional astronomers in Victoria, British Columbia during the summer of 1968. When word spread of UFO activity above the hotel where a reception was going on, not one astronomer went outside to look. It was like the Marx brothers running for cover.

"The first requirement of a scientist," the great quantum physicist Erwin Schrodinger had once said, "is that he be curious. He should be capable of being astonished and eager to find out."

Regarding this incident in British Columbia, Hynek wrote in *The UFO Experience: A Scientific Inquiry*: "The scientific world has sure not been 'eager to find out' about the UFO phenomenon and has expressed no inclination to astonishment. . . . The emotionally loaded, highly exaggerated reaction that has generally been exhibited by scientists to any mention of UFOs might be of considerable interest to psychologists.

"The reaction has been akin to that of a group of pre-teenagers watching a movie scene of exceptional tenderness or pathos quite beyond their years: giggles and squirming suggest a defense against something the scientists cannot yet understand.

"The public," Hynek concluded, "from whom the support of all scientific endeavor ultimately must come, should be given the chance to see science as an adventure pursued in humility of spirit. . . . In science one never knows where inquiry will lead . . . Kuhn has commented that scientific progress tends to be revolutionary rather than evolutionary. . . . When the long awaited solution to the UFO problem comes, I believe it will prove to be not merely the next small step in the march of science but a mighty and totally unexpected quantum leap."

In other words the world view, or paradigm, of most of our scientists is too limited to address the UFO phenomenon.

In all fairness to my colleagues, however, I must acknowledge Hynek's remark that "UFO stories are really so bizarre and unbelievable in everyday terms that it was quite natural for scientists to reject them. They are used to battling crackpots and pseudo-science on an almost daily basis!" But there was a baby in the UFO bath water and Hynek had the courage and integrity to find it.

Hynek's basic views are shared by Jacques Vallee, another UFO researcher with impeccable credentials. "Isn't it interesting," he noted in *The Edge of Reality*, co-authored with Hynek, "that most of my colleagues pick one case here and one case there. . . . They will ignore 15,000 cases because of that one particular case they know. Their landlady said she saw something and they went outside and it was Venus, so that explains everything as far as they are concerned!"

According to Hynek and Vallee, about one in five sightings and/or alleged encounters reported result in a true UFO report, that is, unexplained by conventional means. The many thousands of cases on file constitute a powerful data bank. "We feel it necessary," wrote Vallee in 1965, "to impress on our reader, in advance, the high degree of consistency and reliability of UFO data. . . . There must exist a common cause that has produced all these effects. In my opinion, there are reasons to think that this cause may be related to, or a manifestation of, extraterrestrial intelligence."

After an exhaustive search of the literature on strange encounters throughout history, Vallee has somewhat shifted ground in his recent book *Dimensions*: Such complex and baffling phenomena may be due to the manifestation of an intelligence which may not be conventionally extraterrestrial in the ordinary sense of the term, but is able to move in and out of dimensions beyond space and time. Here inner and outer space truly converge!

Vallee uses these UFO data to outline the search for new paradigms of reality. "Our national science effort," he said, "has temporarily run out of objectives that can capture the public imagination and enthusiasm. . . . While science consistently refuses to consider phenomena that lie outside the safe regions of its current understanding, the public is eagerly reaching for explanations that fit its experience."

In other words, the public is way ahead of its scientists, the non-tabloid media, and the policy of the government. Gallup polls through the years show a steady increase in Americans' belief that UFOs are real: from 40% in 1966 to 54% in 1974 to 60% in 1980 to 80% in 1984. One out of ten people claim to have been witness to UFO phenomena; the actual numbers may be higher when we consider many individuals who have had experiences suppressed, experiences which may come out only after deep reflection or hypnosis. Perhaps *all* of us have had some sort of UFO experience and repressed it.

Meanwhile, allegations of a massive government cover-up appear to take on more and more credibility. As Hynek put it, "To me, it is inconceivable that in any government like ours, which spends so much on intelligence work, somebody wouldn't be interested in this. I approach it from this angle rather than trying to get proof (of a cover-up)."

Ever since the Pentagon put the lid on information after the fateful event in Roswell over forty years ago, the United States Government has repeatedly formed committees with scientists and military personnel specifically to downplay and contradict the validity of UFO phenomena. Such Government-supported projects as Sign, Grudge, Blue Book, and the Condon Report all attempted to turn the public and scientists away from UFOs. And most recently, a number of seemingly legitimate Government reports bearing on the true nature of UFOs have begun to be released under the Freedom of Information Act. Some of these are well-documented in a 1984 book *Clear Intent* by Lawrence Fawcett and Barry Greenwood, with more reports being released in recent years.

Apparently, since 1950, UFO information has been classified "above top secret." Allegations of what the Central Intelligence Agency knows, and the power it wields over how the information is handled, are extraordinary. We have a potential cover-up scandal that would make Watergate and Irangate seem like walks in the park.

One so-called "leaked government document" describes efforts of a top secret "government within the government" to collaborate with the aliens. A recent unpublished report prepared by pilot-entrepreneur John Lear outlines actual steps the Government may have taken to preserve secrecy. According to Lear, the aliens agreed in 1964 to provide us with information on their technology in exchange for continued secrecy about abductions. The plan didn't go well for the Government and in 1979 an alleged showdown between aliens and a special Armed Forces unit resulted in many deaths. Would it be far-fetched to imagine we are ignorant and shortsighted enough to ask the aliens to fund the Contras first, and tell us who they are, afterwards?

Presidents from Truman to Bush apparently have known about many of these things and have been sworn to secrecy. Truman is said to have set up an elite committee of twelve top government officials, military personnel, and scientists to direct UFO policy issues. It was named the Majestic Twelve (MJ-12). Physicist Stanton Friedman, an experienced UFO investigator, is currently researching the activities of the alleged MJ-12.

The Lear report included some rather gruesome interpretations that the intentions of the alleged aliens are a threat to all of us. According to Lear, that is why the intelligence community within the Government has kept it a secret. But things apparently didn't work out as planned. "In its efforts to protect democracy," Lear stated, "our government has sold us to the aliens." He speculated that the Strategic Defense Initiative "Star Wars" program is not intended for the United States to defend against a Soviet nuclear attack but rather against an alien attack!

These conclusions might explain statements made by former president Ronald Reagan just before leaving office: "I've often wondered," he said, "what if all of us in the world discovered that we were threatened by . . . a power in outer space, from another planet? Wouldn't we all of a sudden find that we didn't have any differences at all, we were human beings, citizens of the world, and wouldn't we come together to fight that particular threat?"

Space invaders! Was this a calculated leak revealing the true nature of government intentions? Reagan made similar remarks to Soviet leader Mikhail Gorbachev. But his (and Lear's) scenario of addressing this "hypothetical threat" is more reminiscent of a Western or war movie than an encounter with multi-dimensional beings. It might be like aborigines using slingshots against a Boeing 747. Does Reagan know something we don't? And if he knows, did he lack the vision to provide a more appropriate response?

The apparent policy of Presidential secrecy in the face of incredible implications would explain former President Carter not honoring his campaign pledge to make UFO information public after he took office. Some investigators, including Lear, have even speculated that the assassination of John F. Kennedy was to prevent him from revealing UFO secrets to the public. After testifying to Congress and otherwise being outspoken about government UFO coverups, physicist James McDonald of the University of Arizona was found dead in 1971 under mysterious and unexplained circumstances. A suicide?

We do not know the truth behind the UFO enigma. We do know, however, that the Government has been holding secrets about something from the public, although we do not even know what those secrets are. We do not know what is information, what is supposition, and what is intentional disinformation; hence there remain grounds for speculation. Timely reporting that updates this extraordinary situation can be found in the informative bimonthly magazine *UFO*.

Meanwhile, the UFO investigative community outside the Government is in disarray. Over the past several years, investigators have been at each other's throats in bitter competition to coopt and interpret the best cases. Amateurism and short-sighted egos threaten the credibility of all cases in the public eye. Traditional scientists, the Government, and mainstream media are better able to maintain a lack of UFO credibility when equivalent pot shots fly within the UFO research community.

Perhaps the most famous recent case is that of Ed Walters, a successful businessman from Gulf Breeze, Florida. He has taken about thirty-five high-quality pictures of UFOs over a period of several months using a variety of cameras. He has also reported many encounter experiences, such as being paralyzed and lifted by a blue beam emanating from a craft, hearing voices in his head, and missing time.

Bruce Maccabee, one of the most reputable and experienced UFO investigators, has shared with me the details of the Ed Walters case. Mark Carlotto and I have done some digital processing of the pictures and find they show no indication of faking. These are also Maccabee's conclusions. On the other hand, imaging experts at the Jet Propulsion laboratory suspect that one or two of the pictures might have been faked. If this case were a hoax it would have to be one of the most elaborate in history. Dozens of eyewitnesses in Gulf Breeze have also reported sightings on over fifty-two occasions, giving further credibility to the case.

Budd Hopkins, an artist, hypnotist and abductee authority, has interviewed abductees and revealed a pattern in which women have been artificially inseminated by the aliens, become pregnant, had the embryos removed and taken away in the third month. In his best-selling book *Intruders* he talks about how aliens may have used men and women to create hybrid beings. "Either (the abduction reports) represent some new and heretofore unrecognized and nearly universal psychological phenomenon," he said, "a theory which does not take into account the accompanying *physical* evidence—or they represent honest attempts to report real events." Hopkins laments the enormous emotional suffering experienced by the abductees.

Astronauts have allegedly encountered UFOs throughout the history of manned space flight, according to former NASA officials and reported in Hynek and Vallee's book. The latest incident, just months ago, was betrayed by the following succinct quote, ignored by NASA and the press: "Houston, this is *Discovery*. We still have alien spacecraft under observance." This tidbit was a radio communication during the March 1989 flight of the space shuttle recorded by a ham radio operator.

During the late 1960s while I was a NASA astronaut, I had no knowledge of astronauts' UFO sightings. My enduring friendship with one of the astronauts who had been reported to have had a sighting did not seem to matter when I asked him about whether he had: He was conspicuously evasive. Have the astronauts been sworn to secrecy? Was this the main reason why all of us astronauts—civilians included—had to have top secret clearances? If so, this situation has put the UFO observers into the hot seat with respect to the Government—not an enviable position.

What is happening here? Is there anything within our human power to make sense of all this? At the moment, the experts say no. It appears that, at least in the case of UFOs, most of us do not yet have the psychological equipment to make the necessary paradigm shift. I am a case in point. I ignored UFO data for twenty years as a Ph.D. astronomer. Even when I became open to the information I still found myself resisting in various ways. My mind could not immediately grasp the greater reality nor could it comprehend what that reality might be. It needed time to gestate into acceptance and it now humbly awaits a greater understanding. When I started my UFO research in earnest, poring over case study after case study, I found peculiar things happening to me. I frequently "spaced out" or became irritable as I began to digest the material. I do not know why this was so.

I am not the only one feeling uneasy about UFOs. Abductees, investigators and the informed but puzzled public are going through many of the same feelings of frustration and suppression. Two of my friends with particularly strong psychic powers, when viewing the October 1988 television special "UFO Coverup? Live" mysteriously fell asleep as the astounding, weird information poured forth under loud patriotic sounding music. Were there also subliminal "sleep learning" messages under the distracting music? If so, who would want to do that and why?

We need a transition period in which to become initiated to the UFO reality. But initiated we will almost certainly be. "The human race itself is becoming extraterrestrial," said futurist and friend Barbara Hubbard, "and as we mature, going into the universe physically, and as we also mature in our consciousness, becoming more sensitive to the patterns of evolution and creation and activating our extrasensory dimensions, we will find that we can pick up information from beings of other realities."

There is no doubt, in my opinion, that we are entering the paranormal realms when we deal with UFO encounters. In Chapter 9 we will explore the immense range of paranormal phenomena, some of which are related to UFOs. Certain of these events are subject to scientific inquiry. As our research on UFOs and the paranormal in general progresses, the questions change. No longer are we confined to the old realities of seeking proof, of convincing traditional scientists and a skeptical press. No longer are we concerned about locating the coordinates and characteristics of physical entities. These paranormal phenomena do not appear to operate by such rules.

In our attempts to understand UFOs, we appear to be dealing with paranormal events involving a complex hierarchy of intelligent beings who inhabit levels of reality that occasionally can be experienced by some of us but that are not yet understood. The contacts are not overt; otherwise we would expect a landing on the White House lawn or a Saganesque SETI response.

We need a paradigm larger than our current science, one that might apply as well to our own altered states of consciousness or to the mystical experiences of the masters of the Far East, or to the multi-dimensionality of our quantum mechanics, relativity, and string theory.

Jacques Vallee has speculated that UFO events have "had an impact on a part of the human mind we have not discovered. I believe that the UFO phenomenon is one of the ways through which an alien form of intelligence of incredible complexity is communicating with us *symbolically*. . . . It has access to psychic processes we have not yet mastered or even researched."

The UFO phenomenon is becoming an integral part of our quest for a modern mythology. UFOs may be providing an archetypal symbol of the next step in our spiritual growth. Who said we should expect to have expressed to us our first contact with alien intelligence by radio waves or by encountering spaceships resembling our own or those of conventional science fiction?

The evidence points to UFOs manifesting throughout history. As Vallee points out, UFO phenomena include the visions of Ezekiel in the *Bible*, the fairy rings, and the miracle of Fatima (a "spinning sun" witnessed in 1918 by 70,000 people and felt to be connected to an apparition of the Virgin Mary). Since we are now in the space age and our culture makes its own version of spacecraft, it is only natural for us to make extraterrestrial ships a focus of our attention. Still the phenomenon may be far more complex. We will need to go back into history to understand UFOs more completely.

"If the world around us is a world of informational events," said Valle, "the symbolic manifestations that surround UFO reports should be viewed as an important factor. If we regard the physical world as an associative universe of informational events, consciousness is no longer simply a local function in the human brain. Instead, I propose to define consciousness as the process by which informational associations are retrieved and traversed. The illusion of time and space would be merely a side effect of consciousness as it traverses associations. In such a theory, apparently paranormal phenomena like remote viewing and precognition would be expected, even common, and UFOs would lose much of their bizarre quality. These phenomena would be natural aspects of the reality of human consciousness. I submit that reports of alien 'contact' must be studied at this level, even if we are a long, long way from being able to channel our speculations into the formal equations of a new physics."

We may have flattered ourselves to think that we have mapped where such UFO beings come from within the physical cosmos, yet this merely distracts us from an essence which is yet to be understood. The beings we see may be galactic citizens who are able to move through dimensions of which most of us are unaware. But we must ask ourselves: Does it matter so much where they are from or what their bodies look like or whether they momentarily appear as physical, or astral, or etheric? Does it make that much difference whether their acts seem hostile or friendly, or whether they may be collaborating with the CIA or the MJ-12? Or underneath all these appearances, can we search for a greater essence about themselves and ourselves?

In addition, physical bodies and physical locations begin to lose their traditional significance in the face of advanced genetic engineering, reincarnation, out-of-body experiences, and near death experiences (to be discussed in Chapter 9). Perhaps with UFOs, we are seeing a manifestation of symbols from another spiritual realm teaching us a lesson, symbols that appear as mirrors for our evolution into an expanded awareness beyond the five senses and logical brain. We can better understand the UFO phenomenon if we better understand other aspects of our new reality: the new physics, the paranormal, and metaphysical principles.

Four Approaches to Future UFO Research

We still remain in the dark about the true nature of UFOs and we must therefore continue to probe. In an interview with my friends Brian Myers and Tina Choate, directors of the International Center for UFO Research, founded in 1984 by Allen Hynek, I learned of four approaches that appear to be more promising than the main method of data collection currently being used by most of the UFO research community.

The first approach is simply to *measure* the physical manifestations of UFOs. To accomplish that, the researchers are designing a multispectral analyzer that would pick up signals coming from UFOs, including the electromagnetic spectrum (gamma rays, ultraviolet, visible and infrared light), gravitometers, geiger counters, electrostatic and magnetic field detectors, and ultrasonic detectors. These would be contained in a portable observatory called the Aerial Sensing, Tracking, and Relay Apparatus (Astra). This compact laboratory is named after the Roman goddess of truth and light and resembles R2D2 of the *Star Wars* trilogy. Astra would activate certain of its cameras when any of its detectors saw an anomaly in one or more of its sensors. When the system is set in locations where frequent sightings have taken place, the goal is to provide photographic evidence of UFOs in the context of a fuller range of physical effects.

We do know of many bizarre physical manifestations that take place around supposed UFO craft, but what are they and what causes them? One interesting working hypothesis is that the extra dimensions implied by UFOs are contained within tiny invisible black holes, around which visible, physical phenomena take place. Just as Stephen Hawking and the astronomers are searching interstellar space for physical effects that black holes might have on surrounding objects (for example, relativistic distortions of light by gravity, red shifts, etc.), we can search the neighborhood of photographed or sighted UFOs for similar phenomena. Then we can see if the observations match the predictions.

The second approach for future UFO research is psychological, involving the investigation of the complex experience of those who have undergone a contact, abduction, or sighting. How does the phenomenon affect them? How does it change their world view? "Many of these people begin new quests," said Myers, "becoming more attuned to nature and to the paranormal." Are these the secondary effects of contact, or the primary effects of their subliminal messages?

The third area is social and cultural. "How do UFOs affect cultures at the time?" Myers asked. "How do various groups react such as the scientists, government, and religions? How do cultures incorporate the experience?" It is hard to understand what is happening physically without simultaneously understanding the biases of a given group mind. The same mysterious aspects produce denial at one end of the spectrum and religious cults at the other. Neither serves scientific inquiry.

The fourth area is developing the framework for useful dialogue with the alleged aliens. This is part of a process of maturing mentally and emotionally to embrace the greater reality. We need to prepare, because the day may well come. Our preparation involves all of the above aspects: physical, psychological, and cultural. According to this approach, we must become aware that we are universal citizens, not only citizens of this Earth.

What we need is more than a mental understanding of, and an emotional adjustment to, this phenomenon. We need a broader spiritual perspective. We are already linking the small patch of Western science to patches of Eastern mysticism and other elements of a greater reality to find a common pattern in the fabric of the universe.

Perhaps no area of research is more in need of new scientists than that of UFOs. The work of the scientist is to take apparently disconnected observations and to fit them into a broader, consistent framework or paradigm. The new insight allows us to focus more easily and to develop the necessary tools for understanding.

We are opening a doorway to new dimensions, the contents of which are flooding our unconscious imaginations. "Something is here," wrote Whitley Strieber, "be it a message from the stars or from the labyrinth of the mind . . . or from both . . . And we will all go down the labyrinth, to meet whatever meets us there."

Make no mistake: the imagination is only a part of the new reality. The new science is providing us with a physically tangible pathway toward something so unimaginably immense and significant that we are as adolescents about to be initiated into a seeming infinity.

Bibliography

Andrews, George C., *Extra-Terrestrials Among Us*, Llewelyn, St. Paul, NM (1986).

Aime, Michel, *Flying Saucers and the Straight-Line Mystery*, Criterion, New York (1958).

Berlitz, Charles and William C. Moore, *The Roswell Incident*, Grosset and Dunlap, New York (1980).

Fawcett, Laurence and Barry J. Greenwood, *Clear Intent*, Prentice Hall (1984).

Hall, Richard, *Uninvited Guests*, Aurora Press, Santa Fe, NM (1988).

Hopkins, Budd, *Intruders*, Random House, New York (1987).

Hubbard, Barbara Marx, interview with *UFO*, Vol. 2, No. 2, p. 21 (1987).

Hynek, J. Allen, *The UFO Experience: A Scientific Inquiry*, Ballentine, New York (1972).

Hynek, J. Allen and Jacques Vallee, *The Edge of Reality*, Regnery, Chicago (1979).

Hynek, J. Allen, interview with *Omni* (March 1985).

Kehoe, Donald E., *Aliens from Space*, Doubleday, NY (1973).

Maccabee, Bruce, "A history of the Gulf Breeze, Florida Sightings," presented to the June MUFON Symposium (1988).

Schroedinger, Erwin, *Nature and the Greeks*, Cambridge University Press, Cambridge, England (1954).

Sprinkle, R. Leo, "The changing message of UFO activity: From empirical science to experiential science?" in *Paranormal Research*, edit. by M. Albertson, D. Ward and K. Freeman, Rocky Mountain Institute, Ft. Collins, CO, p. 747 (1988).

Stevens, Wendelle C., *UFO Contact from the Pleiades*, Stevens, Tucson, AZ (1978).

Strieber, Whitley, *Communion*, Morrow, New York (1987).

Strieber, Whitley, *Transformation*, Morrow, New York (1988).

The UFO Phenomenon, by the editors of Time-Life, *Mysteries of the Unknown*, Time-Life Book Series, (1987).

Vallee, Jacques, *UFOs in Space*, Ballentine, New York (1965).

Vallee, Jacques, *Dimensions*, Ballentine, New York (1988).

7

THE LIVING EARTH AND ITS MONUMENTS

> The earth is alive: living, breathing, pulsing . . the "earth mysteries" are becoming part of present day reality, a present-day magical technology. And yet we must beware: we must preserve the sense of mystery, of wonder, or we will lose all sense of meaning with it, and possibly ourselves as well.
>
> —Tom Graves, *Needles of Stone*

> Just as the shell is part of a snail, so the rocks, the air and the oceans are part of Gaia.
>
> —James Lovelock, *The Ages of Gaia*

While UFOs remain on the fringes of palpability and we are still not sure whether or not Mars has ancient stone monuments, we do have some real stone shapes on this planet that suggest an ancient and alien science. Recent measurements of the energies emanating from these sites suggest that the Earth itself is alive and may even be trying to communicate with us. In a sense, the new reality of a planetary consciousness is really an old reality understood by cultures we have disdained as prescientific.

Over the past few years, I have travelled to some of the great megaliths of the Earth: the pyramids of Egypt and Mexico, the astronomical arrays of England and Ireland, the Incan fortresses of Peru, the statues of Easter Island, and the stone slab in the Forbidden City in Beijing, China.

The value of the quest to me, besides sheer joy and awe, was my scientific inquiry that transcended the assumptions of the archaeologists. Was there something these sacred sites had in common that defied mundane, logical explanation? Had the archaeologists literally left the stones unturned?

Paranormal Mechanics

At the risk of sounding naive and unprofessional, I must state the obvious here: There appears thus far to be little or no evidence, nor a scientifically plausible explanation, for how these gigantic stones at all these sites were moved from quarries and erected onto their final positions. In all locales the stones weighed up to about 50 tons, requiring the equivalent of at least 100 "grunters" and "sweaters" to heave-ho across miles of terrain, without the assistance of any modern technology.

Much has been written about the construction of the large pyramids of Giza, Cheops and Kephren. Although the evidence is contradictory, archaeologists tend to agree that the great pyramid was built during the 23-year reign of Cheops. To do the job manually would have required 150,000 men sliding 2,500,000 blocks weighing two to fifty tons each up smooth gradual ramps. The question remains, was that the way it was done?

Peter Tompkins, author of *Secrets of the Great Pyramid*, argues that the means of transporting and placing the pyramid blocks is still not known. I.E.S. Edwards of the Egyptian Department of the British Museum agrees. According to Tompkins, Edwards "spent a lifetime going over the available evidence (of how the pyramids were built). He points out in his scholarly treatise on the pyramids . . . that little or no light is thrown on the subject by extant Egyptian records, either written or pictorial."

"Cheops" wrote Edwards, "who may have been a megalomaniac, could never, during the reign of 23 years, have erected a building of the size and durability of the Great Pyramid if technical advances had not enabled his masons to handle stones of very considerable weight and dimension."

About a hundred years ago, the British surveyor Sir William Petrie, who also studied the pyramids most of his life, pointed out that "in the pyramid of Kephren there is a granite portcullis weighing about two tons which is in such a position in a narrow passage that only six or eight men could work on it at once. As it would take a force of 40 to 60 men to manipulate such a mass, Petrie concludes that Egyptians must have had some more efficient means which remains unknown to us." Tompkins' book contains more such examples.

But the mystery of how these energy requirements were satisfied is not just a historical curiosity. Many of my friends travelling to Egypt have had extraordinary experiences at the pyramids. In March 1985 I decided myself to join a group of spiritually-inclined tourists. Just before sunrise on the day of the vernal equinox, four of us climbed to the top of the great pyramid of Giza. On the way up I felt an invisible push preventing me from ascending the giant steps as fast as I would normally be able to.

On top of the pyramid, even though the ascent was difficult, I felt a sense of awe and wonder as the sun rose. During the rest of the day, I sensed a strong tingling in my scalp, an experience I was later to intuit was the opening of my crown chakra.

Only one time before had I recalled having a similar experience, a few years prior in the Grand Tetons. One beautiful fall day, I had allocated three hours to hike up to Amphitheater Lake and return to the parking lot. While the ranger had told me the round trip would take me at least six hours, I realized that I couldn't do it without missing my flight out. Three hours it had to be. Much to my amazement I succeeded with plenty of time to spare. Not being in that good shape, I somehow managed to climb along the trail, ascending over three thousand feet, feeling a sense of lightness almost as if I were being levitated to the lake. Not only had I made it up there in less than half the time it would normally take for a fit person, but I had twenty minutes alone at the lake to experience the grandeur of the mountains. I noticed that the peaks emanated a peculiar white light. I felt euphoric as I walked leisurely down the mountain with plenty of time to spare.

The Pyramids remain mysterious monuments built by a culture whose abilities certainly exceed what they were credited with by the mainstream archaeologists. The mathematical precision of the Pyramids' proportions and their accurate astronomical alignments suggest a sophisticated culture. Were they simply tombs for megalomaniac pharaohs? Or, were they initiation chambers for individuals seeking to travel out of their physical bodies, as some researchers have speculated? How did the Egyptians have the knowledge and technology to build these things? Was a higher power or other dimensional life involved? These questions could result in volumes of speculation, and yet we still do not have solid answers.

Meanwhile, some 10,000 miles away on the other side of the Earth, small, isolated Easter Island is home to some six hundred stone statutes carved from its quarry between 1100 and 1700 A.D., probably by Polynesians who had migrated there beginning 900 years ago. The weights of these stones are in the range of fifty tons each.

How these remarkable statues were made is no mystery: we see them at various phases of completion at the quarry itself along with an abundance of stone chisels. But how could they have been transported several miles to their end points and then erected on their platforms?

Some archaeologists have speculated that a combination of expert tooling, man-power, logs, rope, and levers could have done the job. Others have argued that this would not be possible because the statues would have been worn down in the moving and/or the balancing would have had to be too delicate. The conventional explanation seems to represent more of a Western scientific approach plus a lot of hard work in sharp contrast to the more relaxed yet spiritual attitude (one that might "move mountains") of the Polynesians. And again we have no direct evidence whatever for how the stones may have been moved.

Similar mysteries surround the construction of the enormous Incan stone walls near Cusco, Peru, and Lake Titicaca. These stones were chiseled to precise sizes and fitted together like a jigsaw puzzle to a precision less than a millimeter between the rocks. They weigh up to several hundred tons. How could they have been cut and carried?

In China, sometime during the Ming Dynasty five hundred years ago, a huge stone slab weighing three hundred tons was quarried and transported for miles to the Forbidden City in Beijing. This exquisitely carved slab ascends three flights of stairs. Nobody knows how it was moved.

And, of course, there are the stone megaliths of Great Britain and Ireland. At Stonehenge, stones weighing as much as fifty tons were erected about 3000 to 5000 years ago. The great stone monuments of the world have in common the mystery of how they may have been moved into place. Their construction predated Newton's mechanics that brought us levers and pulleys. Even modern cranes and bulldozers would have had extreme difficulty in doing the job in some instances.

Could gravity have been temporarily suspended and the stones levitated by the group's energy? Perhaps the stones were moved as effortlessly as I glided up the hill of yet another sacred site that Fall in the Tetons. We will return to the questions of levitation in Chapter 9, in which I present modern evidence for psychokinesis.

Do these monuments also have some relationship to the enormous face and pyramids that might be present on Mars? Did an advanced culture build on both planets?

The Dragon Project

All this is interesting speculation, but the role that science was to take in confronting these mysteries began to change in 1977. An interdisciplinary team began to measure the energies emanating from the megaliths of Britain. Calling their work the Dragon Project, and operating with only paltry funding, this collection of physicists, chemists, electronics engineers, dowsers, geologists, historians, a trance-psychic, an astrologer, a folklore researcher, and a zoologist deployed an extraordinary variety of instruments to test the theory that the sacred sites do in fact contain special energies.

Dr. Don Robins, a specialist in archeological chemistry, measured unexpected pulses with an ultrasonic detector and geiger counters at the Rollright stone circle near Oxford. Ultrasonics refer to those high pitched sounds beyond our hearing range while geiger counters measure the decay of radioactive materials such as uranium as well as the background of galactic cosmic rays. The results seemed so bizarre and difficult to interpret that Robins, himself a traditional scientist, wrote a book *Circle of Silence* describing the mysterious results and how they challenged conventional scientific thinking.

Robins measured unusual ultrasonic pulsings around the stone circle at Rollright that occurred only for an hour or two after dawn during the months around the spring and fall equinoxes. He also discovered a high radiation zone near one of the standing stones. Perhaps most mysterious of all was the radiation reading inside several of the stone circles which was lower than the cosmic background. In other words, the stones at the sites somehow managed to shield the instrument from its normal readings of cosmic rays impinging on the surface of the Earth. This finding has been repeated many times since.

"There seem to be anomalies at the circles," Robins concluded, "which are not apparent at a very wide range of control sites. It may be a factor in the earth, it may be a consequence of the evolution of the stones, it may be a conjunction of the two factors. Either way, we are led to think that, somehow and at some level, the megalith builders had an awareness of the phenomenon . . . (which) cannot be perceived by our unaided sensory system. If the anomalies are attributes of some more fundamental feature, then that, too is likely to be beyond our limits of direct perception, unless we suggest that it is accessible to some form of heightened awareness."

Robins was careful to point that this "does not necessarily conflict with the findings of orthodox archeology; nor do we discredit either the geometric or astronomical lobbies by incorporating energy anomaly aspects into the overall picture. They can all coexist, even though the new recruit does make life a little uncomfortable for the established members!"

But there is much more to this. Using improved equipment, electronics designer Rodney Hale measured strong correlations between anomalous radio signals (part of the electromagnetic spectrum) and the geiger readings (atomic decay) at Rollright. And there was total radio silence—no background noise at all—at two megalithic sites in Ireland, Newgrange and Loughcrew. Such readings are theoretically impossible in the absence of human-created shields. What was happening here?

In the summer of 1988 I visited the Newgrange site. It includes a large, well-preserved burial mound with surrounding stone megaliths, all believed to be constructed over 5000 years ago. The corridor to the central chamber is aligned to the winter solstice sunrise for a precious few moments of full illumination. I had the opportunity to sit in the central chamber of the mound and meditate for a few minutes. Never in my life have I felt such a sensation of silence. My ears filled with a humming that became a beautiful vibration that sent my head into a feeling of expanded awareness.

The silence I felt was consistent with an attempt by a psychically gifted student to "tune in" to the music played at ancient ceremonies as part of a thesis for which Robins—the "hard" scientist—was advisor. "The basis of the dissertation," wrote Robins, "was that, despite a vivid 'psychic access' to the neolithic gatherings, the ceremonies appeared to be held in total silence."

Perhaps the silence permitted them a form of inter-dimensional awareness and immortality. Perhaps these qualities crossed cultures into Egypt, Peru, North America, China, and elsewhere. Maybe *we* are the ones living in the darkness of our ignorance. Maybe *we* are the ones trapped in a belief of our own mortality.

The Dragon project magnetometer also measured some strange pulsings at the Rollright site, with the most anomalous of all occurring at stone 62. One day during a survey the magnetic field at the site suddenly increased by a factor of thousands for no apparent reason. In January 1986 the Dragon project scientists observed a flame-type spark discharge from the top of the stone, an event which project director Paul Devereaux was able to photograph with his camera. Evidently, these unusual energies detected at the stone circles are physical but they may also be non-physical. Certainly their origin is as undisclosed to us as that of UFOs.

Dowsing and Ley Lines

Understanding the living Earth is a direct scientific pathway to the greater reality. The anomalous ultrasonic, radio, geiger, and magnetometer readings just mentioned are well-documented in thousands of controlled experiments. What could be going on?

During the 1920s and 1930s Alfred Watkins discovered that the sacred sites fell along straight paths that crisscrossed the countryside; he called these ley lines. The more complex sites had been constructed on the intersections of the lines.

An art known as dowsing has been used to measure some of the unusual energy patterns found at these sites. Dowsing makes use of rods or sticks, or even the human hand, to sense the presence of a number of things: underground water, minerals, energy fields of objects and living things, and the kind of energy anomalies that take place at the stone megaliths. Depending on the experience of dowsers, this tool can be very useful and precise in locating water. The working hypothesis here is that there exists an energy interaction between the seeker and the sought that pinpoints the location of the sought by triangulating from points at which a divining rod reacts.

Dowsing is easy for anybody to learn. I have sometimes used a pair of ordinary coat hangers shaped as L's to measure the changing energy levels of people. It did not take me long to learn how to use the rods to detect significant increases of a person's energy field simply as a result of their relaxing, breathing deeply, and having pleasant, loving thoughts. The effect is even more dramatic when I demonstrate this in front of an audience before and after the entire audience is instructed to radiate this "positive energy" for a few seconds to an individual being dowsed. Without exception, an energy field once three to five feet in extent will expand to over twenty feet. We do not know the origin of the effect being measured, but it is consistent with the observations of some clairvoyants and Kirlian photography showing the extended auras of healthy individuals versus the contracted auras of unhealthy people.

The effect can also be observed in water. By blessing one of a large number of identical cups of water and leaving the room to allow another person to switch the cups, I can return and identify the cup of blessed water by dowsing. The blessed water will have a larger energy field and will also taste better in a blindfold test. These are experiments one can learn to do in an hour or two. Even though a neophyte myself, I have taught them to many others. In order for them to work you only need to have a clear and open mind and body. Food and alcohol tend to dampen the effect.

Dowsing works reliably for those able to use it effectively. We can hypothesize that there exists an energy interaction between the dowser and the dowsed that causes the rods to react. We do not know yet what causes that interaction—whether it is a direct physical reaction to an electromagnetic or other physical field—or whether it may be a new kind of field hitherto unknown. Here we are dealing with an unknown science in which experiments clearly show something is happening, but theory has no model. Obviously even the universe of Stephen Hawking is missing key parameters. Mainstream science has all but ignored the significance of dowsing. Yet here we may have an appropriate analogue to the new physics: the observer interacting with the observed. But most scientists don't want to hear that we cannot model the universe with predictable interacting billiard balls, or even quantum ones.

Dowsing gives us valuable information on the energy patterns of the sacred sites and ley lines—their shapes and intensities as a function of time. Dowser Tom Graves integrates this information with the Dragon project results. He notes the frequent appearances of ghosts, ghouls, poltergeists, and UFOs at these places. He also describes "magical" influences people may have around such sites as they contribute to the paranormal phenomena they experience. All these unusual happenings, he feels, somehow relate to the Earth energy flowing underground and overground into the sites.

Dowsers have also discovered that some energy events are correlated with positions of the Sun and Moon as suggested by the well-established astronomical alignments of some of the stone circles. Just as the Rollright stones exhibit anomalous ultrasonic pulses at equinox sunrises, dowsers have found energy bands around most large stones that respond to the phases of the Moon at seven levels. "All seven bands," said Graves, "according to several researchers I've talked to, are tapping points into a spiral release of some kind of energy that moves up and down the stone, following the lunar cycle." We have seen many reports about the influence of a full Moon on the human psyche; these dowsing experiments are consistent with the theory that the Moon's influence on us transcends well-known mechanical effects like the tides.

Graves also sees the megalithic stones as "earth- acupuncture" needles. Just as the Chinese found points on the human body to relieve pressure or blockages building up at intersections along energy lines or meridians, he sees the ley lines as being Earth's energy conduits (water being one manifestation) whose intersections must be periodically cleared. Thus their role as power spots apparently depends on our awareness of their existence and our ability to manipulate the flow of energy through them. Did we once know how to alter the Earth to enhance our harmony with nature? Graves believes so, as do a number of researchers who have revived the ancient Chinese art of geomancy —the use of landscape shapes to create balance with nature. In a recent book, Nigel Pennick describes the significance of geomancy to various cultures through the ages.

"British geomancy," Graves wrote, "if it did exist, would seem to have been a system of earth-acupuncture, with the sacred sites as acupuncture points on energy channels, both sinuous and straight, with the standing stones and the like as massive needles of stone. And if that is the case, we now need to look again at these stones, with a rather different point of view: to put them to *use*, in the present rather than in the past."

Graves' book includes a thorough discussion of possible causes of the paranormal phenomena experienced at the sites, including a holographic theory of ghost projections. He also describes a theory of orgone energy (a life-force energy proposed by the visionary scientist Wilhelm Reich) that may be operating at such sites. According to the theory, when this energy interacts with subsurface water, it could give rise to UFOs, ghosts, crazy weather, and other unusual events being experienced by those in the vicinity. The frequent UFO sightings and encounters over ley lines is consistent with similar results reported by researcher Aime Michel, who noticed that many UFO events in France also happened along straight lines. Yet another researcher, Captain Bruce Cathie, has concluded that UFO sightings form a worldwide grid system. This would suggest a terrestrial rather than an extraterrestrial origin or that extraterrestrial UFOs are using the Earth's ley lines for navigation.

Graves documents people who, in the vicinity of the megalithic stones, have been lifted, thrown back, electrically shocked, terrified by poltergeists, killed in auto accidents created by apparitions, and had encounters with UFOs.

One day last summer, three of us dowsed at a medieval megalithic site on the Dingle peninsula in western Ireland. We measured strong complex energy patterns connected to what the guide book described as a children's graveyard. One half hour into the dowsing session, all three of us suddenly became dizzy and nauseous. We quickly left the site and recovered as soon as we drove away.

Some of us on occasion may experience "bad vibes" at a place. I did once during a visit with a friend to the sacred community of Glastonbury in England. It seemed as if our own darker aspects amplified into a veritable nightmare of emotions which only cleared away when we drove back to London. Only later was I to read in Graves' book that "high energy levels at a place like Glastonbury can make the whole area surrounding it unstable, at an emotional level and beyond . . . The time spent travelling to the place must be a period of contemplation and preparation, or else you won't be able to handle what will be thrown at you by the place." I had not been prepared.

Whatever the scientific explanation of these phenomena may turn out to be, they are obviously real for those experiencing them. Graves believes that the energies transcend those which can be accounted for using the known laws of nature understood by today's physicists, laws that include electromagnetic, gravitational, weak nuclear, and strong nuclear forces. It appears that something is operating whose effects are becoming more evident, but whose causes await the formulation of a new theory.

Perhaps Graves' most encouraging contribution does not concern the phenomena themselves, but how earth-acupuncture techniques can be used to help heal our planet. This may sound far-fetched at first, but experiments have already revealed the usefulness of performing acupuncture at sites that are known to contain negative energies. Dowsers have used stakes and coils to balance the negative energy at people's houses exposed to the energy-matrix of ley lines. Conversely, Graves suggests that shield rings could be placed around certain military installations and political offices so their negative influences could not be felt along the matrix but instead would remain isolated within the ring.

Were the stone circles also rings of protection isolating the participants of a ritual from negative influences of the Earth and sky and from other human beings? Perhaps they would be able to free themselves to travel into other dimensions. Perhaps the function of these megalithic sites and pyramids was to manipulate energies to permit access to the paranormal. We do not know the answer to this because we have not yet learned the nature of the energy or energies involved. Perhaps it's appropriate that we *don't* know, given our rampant misuse of the technology we already have on Earth today.

We know that the human degrading of our land is interfering with the flow of the energy through the megalithic sites. Dowsing measurements have shown that bulldozed sites and fast-moving automobiles disrupt the flow and that the flow begins to restore itself when the land is repaired or the traffic is diverted or slowed down.

It may be possible to reach our next level of development as we begin to understand the workings of this energy emanating from the Earth, from ourselves, and from space. We can manipulate it for our good, although we have unwittingly been doing the opposite. Our focus seems to have been on using our physics-based technology to destroy ourselves and our planet. We are blinded from our own great potential.

"We call such things 'supernatural'," writes Graves, "and say they cannot occur or exist, since they are outside the boundaries of the limited view of nature that science and religion demand. But as we have seen, such things are aspects of the reality of nature: they are not 'unnatural.' What is unnatural is our science, our religion, our politics and economics: for all are carried on in complete and deliberate ignorance of nature, in the belief or hope that nature will conveniently change itself to suit our whims. It gives us a pleasant illusion of control—but it's unnatural, and it's insane, in every sense of the word."

Again, the scientist is in new territory. He must be careful not to embrace without careful examination every new metaphysical concept that comes along. Jumping to conclusions or overinterpreting data can distract him from making relevant contributions to the human condition. He does, however, need to break free of the old world view.

The Interaction of Earth and Celestial Energies

In this chapter I have tried to show how many of our ancient cultures may have been aware that the Earth possesses energies unknown today, and that information is just now being provided by modern scientists using state-of-the-art equipment to prove the existence of such energies. Some of the Earth energies appear to be non-electromagnetic and non-gravitational, and are related to the lunar and solar cycles. If this is the case, could energy impinge on the Earth from celestial bodies in such a way that the sacred sites change their energy output? Was this why those civilizations exercised obvious care to align their stones so they could track the motions of the Sun, Moon, and planets?

If the answer to these questions is yes, this could give some physical basis for the ancient art of astrology. In modern times, astrology has been totally discarded by mainstream science, yet it is practiced by millions, including world leaders. Analyzing the scientific basis for astrology is challenging, for here we must deal with seeming correlations between planetary positions and the individual psyche. For example, we have the well-known high incidence of emergency room admissions at the time of the full Moon. Perhaps we are not only dealing with people interacting with one another, but also with Earth energies responding to lunar and planetary energies. As in Backster's experiments, the hypothesized energy does not appear to be electromagnetic or gravitational.

Astrology might better be explained in terms of Earth consciousness interacting with other planetary consciousness. "Imagine the Earth," said Brian Myers, "to be like a giant head sensing its environment. As it rotates on its axis and travels around the Sun, it senses the presence of the other planets and may actually share a form of communication with them. In other words, the individuals's response to astrological influences might actually be the individual's interaction with the Earth's energies while the Earth, as a planetary entity, is responding to the emanations coming from other celestial bodies." In our new science we would like to be able to measure the emanations.

Gaia and the New Scientist

We have seen that energies from the Earth and sky may be affecting our lives. Furthermore, by many definitions, the Earth can be seen to be alive. In his landmark books, *Gaia* and *The Ages of Gaia*, inventor-scientist James Lovelock advanced the theory that the Earth itself behaves as a self-organizing superorganism. According to Lovelock, many of our support systems hang in a delicate balance that is continuing to be threatened by our environmental pollution—the ravages of forestry, agriculture, acid rain, the depletion of our fragile ozone layer, and the greenhouse effect.

Lovelock cites evidence that the evolution of the various species is tightly coupled with that of their environment; they all evolve as a single system—the Earth. He sees the health of the planet as a primary challenge of our time, stating the need for new fields he calls geophysiology and planetary medicine.

"You may think the academic scientist is the analogue of the independent artist," he writes. "In fact, nearly all scientists are employed by some large organization, such as a government department, a university, or a multinational company. Only rarely are they free to express their science as a personal view. They may think they are free, but in reality they are, nearly all of them, employees; they have traded freedom of thought for good working conditions, a steady income, tenure, and a pension."

Lovelock also laments the scientists' dependence on bureaucratic funding, the constraints of staying within a narrow discipline, and the pressures of peer-review: "Lacking freedom they are in danger of succumbing to a finicky quality or of becoming, like medieval theologians, the creatures of dogma." He then speculates that, had he been working at an institution, his research on a living Earth would certainly not have been funded, nor would it have been condoned by a hypothetical lab director, even if the research had been done on his own time.

"I have had to become a radical scientist," he said, "also because the scientific community is reluctant to accept new theories as fact, and rightly so. It was nearly 150 years before the notion that heat is a measure of the speed of molecules became a fact of science, and 40 years before plate tectonics was accepted by the scientific community.

"Now perhaps you see why I work at home supporting myself and my family by whatever means come to hand. It is no penance, rather a delightful way of life that painters and novelists have always known about. Fellow scientists, join me, you have nothing to lose but your grants." Two years ago, I followed Lovelock's advice. My conscience no longer permitted me to do otherwise.

I believe we cannot any longer afford the luxuries of comfortable old thinking or exhaustive "show-me" proofs. We have a planet to heal, and this includes ourselves, our communities, and our nations. The greater reality becomes not a parlor game for a metaphysical elite, but a necessity.

Bibliography

Bond, Jane and Colin, *Mysterious Britain*, Paladin, London (1974).

Brennan, Martin, *The Stars and the Stones*, Thames and Hudson, London (1983).

Brown, Peter Lancaster, *Megaliths and Masterminds*, Scribner's, New York (1979).

Cathie, Bruce, *Harmonic 33*, Reed, Wellington, Syndey and London (1968).

Devereux, Paul and Paul McCartney, *Earth Lights*, Thorsons, London (1982).

Graves, Tom, *Needles of Stone Revisited*, Gothic Image, Glastonbury, U.K. (1986).

Graves, Tom, *The Diviner's Handbook*, Aquarian Press, Wellingborough, U.K. (1974).

Hitching, Francis, *Earth Magic*, Morrow, New York (1976).

Lovelock, James, *Gaia: A New Look at Life on Earth*, Oxford, NY (1979).

Lovelock, James, *The Ages of Gaia*, Norton, New York and London (1988).

Michel, Aime, *The Truth About Flying Saucers*, Robert Hale, London (1957).

Michell, John, *The New View Over Atlantis*, Thames & Hudson, London (1983).

Mystic Places, Time-Life Book Series "Mysteries of the Unknown," Alexandria, VA (1987).

Pennick, Niguel, *The Ancient Science of Geomancy*, Thames & Hudson, London (1979).

Robins, Don, *Circles of Silence*, Souvenir, London (1985).

Tompkins, Peter, *Secrets of the Great Pyramids*, Harper & Row, New York (1971).

Watson, Lyall, *Supernature*, Hodder & Soughton, London (1973).

8

CONSCIOUSNESS COMMUNICATION AND THE NEW BIOLOGY

> In the holistic model there is much more emphasis on the way that at different levels of complexity nature is organized into what we could call organisms —cells, tissues, organs, societies—and that at each of these levels there's a wholeness which can't be reduced to the sum of the parts. This means that we respect the different levels of organization in nature without trying to reduce them, and also regard nature as in some sense alive, as opposed to being ultimately reducible to particles of matter that are dead. . . . I think the mechanistic and reductionistic ways of understanding are inadequate to solve biological problems. Their medical and social consequences are destructive and their ecological consequences for the Earth actually threaten the survival of our civilization.
>
> —Rupert Sheldrake, *Noetic Sciences Review*

In the opening chapter, I shared my experiences in Cleve Backster's laboratory. They clearly demonstrated to me a relationship between the emotions and thoughts of a person, on the one hand, and the electrical activity of plants and of his own at-a-distance blood cells, on the other hand. Sexual activity appeared to evoke a particularly strong response, irrespective of distance.

These results are consistent with Backster's observation that plants and other living things can be affected by, and act as voyeurs with regard to, human thoughts and emotions, and that sexual energy in particular is strongly communicated. Such findings also concur with research chemist Maurice Vogel's experimental results obtained from plants. They are consistent with Wilhelm Reich's observations of galvanic skin response that show the largest deflections during times of orgasm. Reich concluded that the electrical potential of the skin responded to a life energy he called "orgone energy." Earlier this century, Reich had created quite a stir with his highly controversial work which ended with his untimely death in jail in 1957.

In light of these newer experiments, Reich's work is gaining credibility. His primary hypothesis was that orgone energy is unipolar and fills everything in space and time. When this energy meets a resistance within a person, it splits into two poles, positive and negative. These cause a conflict, duality, sexual repression, and eventual illness if the blocks are not released.

As Vogel put it, "So much of the ills and suffering in life comes from our inability to release stresses and forces within us. When a person rejects us, we rebel inside and we hold on to this rejection. This builds a stress which, as Dr. Wilhelm Reich showed so long ago, becomes locked in as muscular tension, and if not unblocked, depletes the body's energy field and alters its chemistry." These effects are reminiscent of the Earth energies discussed in the last chapter. We shall see in Chapter 10 that the enormous revolution now taking place in the health field involves the principle of unblocking accumulated energy and bathing our cells with positive thinking. Healing has to do with communicating positively with our bodies.

What kind of energy are we dealing with in the case of the paranormal communication in Backster's lab, or with the processes referred to by Reich and Vogel? As one candidate of explanation, we have the familiar forces of the electromagnetic spectrum, spanning from the higher frequencies and shorter wavelengths of the gamma rays, x-rays, and ultraviolet rays to the lower frequencies and longer wavelengths of the visible, infrared and radio waves. But they do not fit the data. One experiment confirming this was carried out by the psychic Ingo Swann at Stanford University. "With nothing but his will power" wrote Tompkins and Bird, "Swann has been able to affect a mechanism in the university's most thoroughly shielded 'quark' chambers, buried deep underground in a vault of liquid helium, impenetrable to any known wavelength of the electro-magnetic spectrum, astonishing the academic physicists who watch him perform what they considered to be an impossible feat."

We need our best theoretical physicists and life scientists to develop a set of hypotheses and theories to explain the panoply of unusual communications among living beings and between them and the Earth. The data are crying out for coherent interpretations. Meanwhile, we stay in confusion within a vague terminology, with many well intentioned New Agers bandying about talk of electromagnetic waves, frequencies, and "vibrations". Our language has yet to catch up with the observed reality.

One pathway toward understanding is a hypothesis advanced by Dr. Rupert Sheldrake, a molecular biologist, formerly director of cell biology and biochemistry at Clare College in Cambridge University. Sheldrake noticed that many living things have a tendency to repeat habits developed by other members of their species without benefit of any direct genetic transfer or environmental learning.

One example of this is the popular fable of the hundredth monkey. This account is based on a report by Japanese anthropologists who observed how monkeys on a given island washed their sweet potatoes. They noticed that one monkey discovered a new method of doing this, and the habit soon spread throughout the island. By the time one hundred monkeys learned the new method, very quickly all monkeys on the adjacent islands began to do it. How the information was communicated from island to island remains a mystery. Although this story has recently been debunked, it gives us a fable for understanding the very real learning processes that occur within groups on such a regular mundane basis they are taken for granted.

Sheldrake notes that habit-forming characteristics apply as well to rats in laboratories throughout the world, to human behavior, and even to new crystal forms that can be more easily synthesized in other laboratories once the first one is synthesized. These phenomena are examples of what he calls "causative formation."

"The hypothesis I'm pushing forward," he said, "suggests that once a certain pattern of behavior or activity or form has got going, it will tend to be repeated—that basically nature is habit forming. The laws of nature may be more like habits than changeless principles that are given from the very beginning." Where the thought or pattern first came from, Sheldrake suggests, is a question for religion to address.

Based on his hypothesis and on supporting experiments, Sheldrake calls into question the existence of unchanging physical forces in nature. "We are so used to the notion of immutable physical laws that we take them for granted;" he pointed out, "but if we pause to reflect on the nature of these laws, they are profoundly mysterious. They are not material things, nor are they energetic. They both transcend space and time, and are at least potentially present in all places and at all times . . . The mechanistic theory depends on assumptions that are, if anything, *more* metaphysical than the idea of formative causation." As we have seen earlier, the new reality does not accept any one law or model as being sacrosanct.

Sheldrake's ideas are consistent with the fact that our current physical laws break down or are incomplete inside the primordial Big Bang, the black holes, quantum wave-particles, and in the mysterious energy exchanges which we see happening so frequently among living entities. We are clearly in need of a new paradigm.

Even if we step back from the revolutionary observations and theories advanced by Backster and Sheldrake we still find abundant evidence of a new biology whose tenets become yet another blow to mainstream science. In a recent book entitled *The New Biology*, Robert Augros and George Stanciu manage to stay close to established academic science and avoid making reference to the controversies surrounding Burr's, Backster's, Vogel's and Sheldrake's work. Even so, they come to a conclusion that is similar to that of these other researchers.

"Contemporary biology", they wrote, "suffers from narrowness because of its strong inclination to various kinds of reductionism. . . . Modern biology, thus unable to distinguish itself from physics, is oddly out of step with modern physics, which has broken the monopoly of mechanistic explanations. . . . Yet another form of narrowness tries to reduce consciousness to physiology. Reductionism is a half truth. . . . With its emphasis on populations and whole environments, the new biology offers an effective antidote to reductionism. In acknowledging purpose and mind, biology can free itself from the tyranny of mechanistic explanations. . . .

Nature . . . is a model for both engineer and artist. Her attributes of simplicity, economy, beauty, purpose and harmony make her a model for ethics and politics. The rediscovery of nature's wisdom calls for a new biology."

Augros and Stanciu document evidence for a cooperative, harmonious biology guided by a higher mind rather than by the ruthless, relentless, and mechanistic survival of the fittest. They also address the question of what constitutes life, noting that biologists do not have a working definition. The mechanistic thinking at the foundation of traditional biology blurs the boundary between life and non-life so that there seems to be no distinction between biology and the other natural sciences. Augros and Stanciu define life as "the capacity for self motion."

James Lovelock was also shocked at the lack of a definition of life among biologists named to search for life on Mars on the 1976 Viking Mission. "I expected to discover somewhere in the scientific literature," he said, "a comprehensive definition of life as a physical process, on which one could base the design of life detection experiments, but was surprised to find how little was written about the nature of life itself. . . . At best, the literature read like a collection of expert reports, as if a group of scientists from another world had taken a television receiver home with them and had reported on it. The chemist said it was made of wood, glass, and metal. The physicist said it radiated heat and light. The engineer said the supporting wheels were too small and in the wrong places for it to run smoothly on a flat surface. But nobody said what it was."

Perhaps the definition of life will need to be expanded to all self-organizing and/or communicating entities in the universe, known and unknown. Clearly, in any case, we are dealing with a different "biology," one that involves intricate combinations of interactions between living systems at many levels of complexity. We need to devise a theory that at bare minimum explains the mysteries of the hundredth monkey syndrome, Sheldrake's theories, Burr's life force measurements, and Cleve Backster's results. How does communication take place among living things in the absence of direct physical and environmental contact and, in some cases, in the absence of the four known forces of physics?

There must exist another force or series of forces of nature whose origin and behavior we do not yet understand; and I believe we have sufficient data we can begin to apply to hypotheses we can advance to explain these forces. Sheldrake has proposed one hypothesis and I imagine there will need to be others that apply to other characteristics besides form and habit.

British researchers David Ash and Peter Hewitt propose that a "super-energy" field creates small electrical impulses in living cells because DNA molecules may resonate with various frequencies directed toward them in the field: "Cells," they say, "could be acting as radio sets, receiving signals from intelligent sources acting like relay stations in the higher realms of the universe. These thought-form signals, setting the fields of life into vibration and resonating with DNA molecules, could be transferred into genetic codes. In this way, universal intelligence could direct the process of biological evolution, via genetic variation, towards increased order and diversity."

This framework would help explain Sheldrake's findings and the surprising orderliness of life systems proposed in the new biology. Ash and Hewitt also point out that our early radios used a helical shape as the resonating crystals. DNA also forms a double helix.

We recall that in string theory, a unified field requires that matter-energy forms tiny strings in ten-dimensional space. Some of these strings also take a helical shape. We have also seen that dowsers have found that the energy coming off the stone megaliths correlated with the lunar cycle take on a helical pattern. Are we involved in some sort of cosmic dance of archetypal helices resonating with some universal life force at various levels of consciousness? Would understanding and manipulating these energies, their patterns and resonances allow us to develop a technology permitting us to enter other dimensions?

This is the kind of adventurous thinking that may be required to develop our new theories of science. Observations are outstripping theory because our theories so far have been limited by the narrow world view of our biology and the limitations of our language. In the next chapter we will find that an understanding of the concept of mind and thought forms may well provide the missing link in formulating a theory of the new reality that bridges inner and outer space by including consciousness itself.

Bibliography

Ash, David and Peter Hewitt, *Science of the Gods*, manuscript (1988).

Augros, Robert and George Stanciu, *The New Biology*, New Science Library, Boston and London (1988).

Burr, Harold Saxon, *Blueprint for Immortality: The Electric Patterns of Life*, Neville Speareman, London (1972).

Cosmic Connections, Time-Life Book series *Mysteries of the Unknown*, Alexandria, Virginia (1987).

Keyes, Ken. Jr., *The Hundredth Monkey*, Vision Books, Coos Bay, Oregon (1986).

Lovelock, James, *Gaia, A New Look At Life on Earth*, Oxford, New York (1979).

Lovelock, James, *The Ages of Gaia*, Norton, New York and London (1988).

Russell, Peter, *The Global Brain*, Tarcher, Los Angeles (1983).

Sheldrake, Rupert, *A New Science of Life*, Tarcher, Los Angeles (1981).

Sheldrake, Rupert, *The Presence of the Past*, Times Books, New York (1988).

Sheldrake, Rupert, interview with David Tapper, Noetic Sciences Review, Spring (1987).

Tompkins, Peter and Christopher Bird, *The Secret Life of Plants*, Harper and Row, New York (1973).

Watson, Lyall, *Lifetide*, Bantam Books, New York (1980).

Variation VI Pleiadian "Beamship" with reported ability to hyper-jump to Pleiades star group in 7 minutes "realtime." Photograph taken by Mr. Eduard Meier in Sekar Durchtrolen, Switzerland, 26 March 1981, printed courtesy of Genesis III by permission of Mr. Lee Elders, July 7, 1989.

Photograph taken at Shoreline Park; Gulf Breeze, Florida, June 1986, by an unidentified female named "Jane." Submitted to Duane Cook of The *Gulf Breeze Sentinel*. Photo reproduction credit, Bob Oechsler.

The author with Whitley Strieber in his upstate New York cabin.

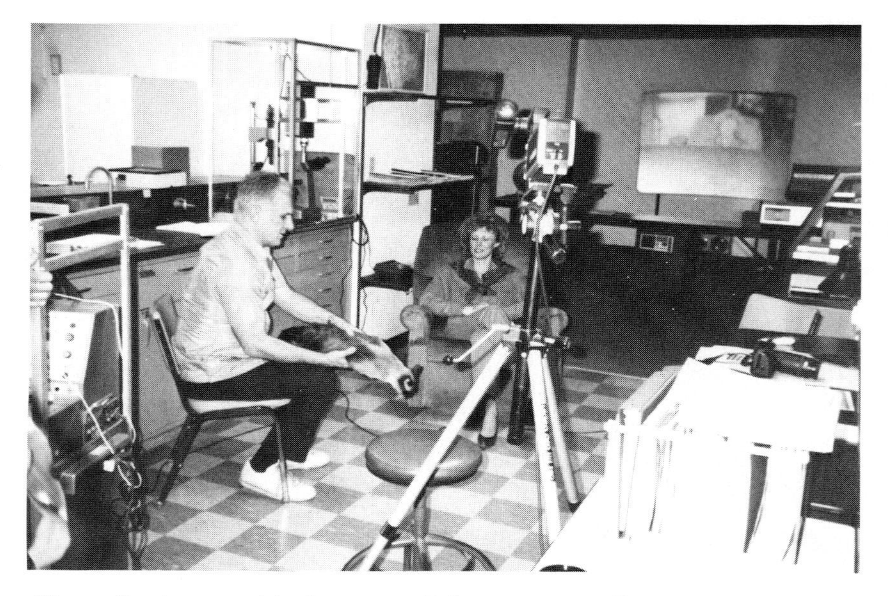

Cleve Backster with Laurene Johnson on split-screen television after donating her white blood cells. The bottom half of the screen shows changes in the electrical current in the cells elsewhere in the laboratory.

The author climbing the Great Pyramid of Egypt at vernal equinox sunrise in 1985.

The author's photographs of Stonehenge, the most famous of the ancient stone megaliths.

The mysterious statues of Easter Island, author in foreground.

The pyramids and cities of the Aztecs at Chichen Itza, Mexico.

This 300-ton stone carving in the Forbidden City in Beijing, China, was somehow moved from its quarry at the time of the Ming Dynasty.

Brian O'Leary and Soviet cosmonaut Vitaly Sevastayanov.

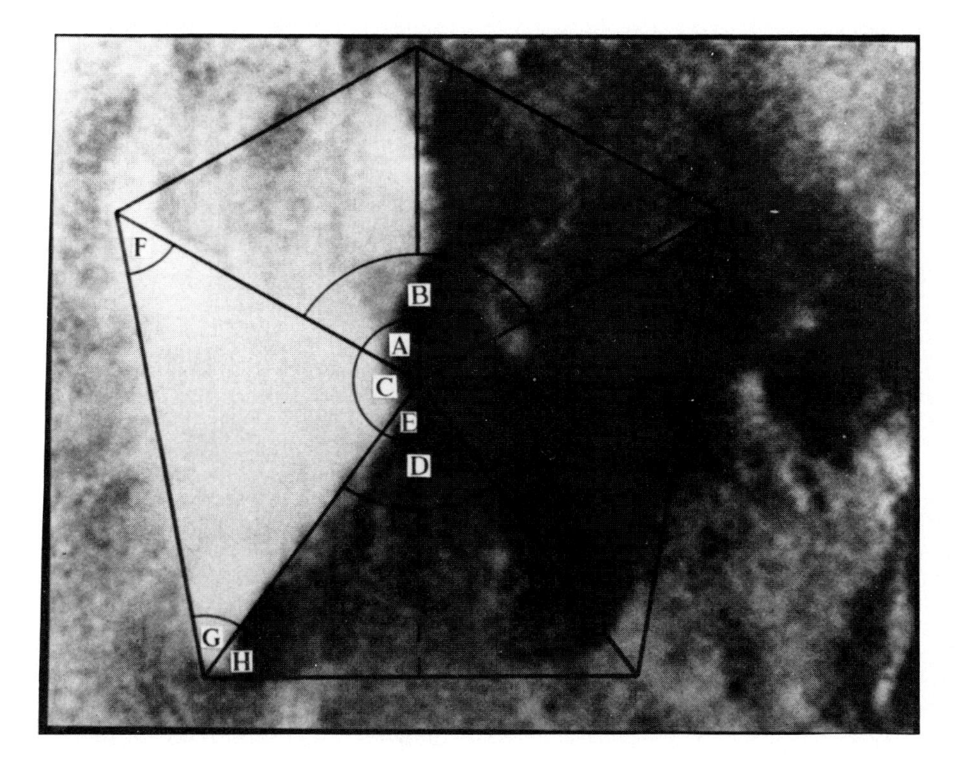

Angles		Angle Ratios	Trig. Functions
degrees	radians		
A = 60.0	= π/3	C/A = √2	TAN A = √3
B = 120.0	= 2π/3	B/D = √3	TAN B = -√3
C = 85.3		C/F = √3	SIN A = e/π
D = 69.4	= e/√5	A/D = e/π	SIN B = e/π
E = 34.7		C/D = e/√5	TAN F = π/e
F = 49.6	= e/π	A/F = e/√5	COS E = √5/e
G = 45.1		H/G = e/√5	SIN G = √5/π
H = 55.3		B/C = π/√5	
		D/F = π/√5	

The so-called "D & M Pyramid" in the Cydonia region of Mars, with angles and functions marked by geomorphologist Erol Torun.

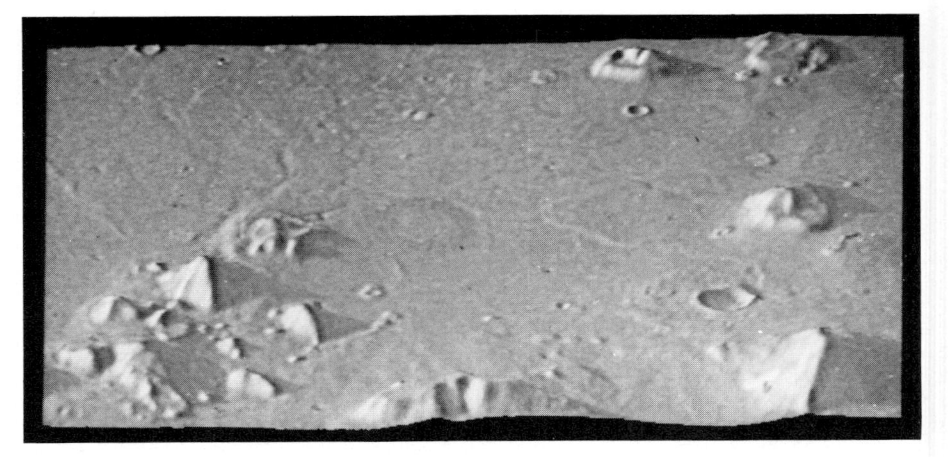

Perspective view of the face on Mars (top right), the "city" (left) and the D & M Pyramid (lower right), looking from the west and well above the Martian surface. Processed by Dr. Mark Carlotto.

The "raw," unprocessed Viking photo 35A72 of the 2-kilometer wide face on Mars and the surrounding terrain. The circle in the upper left corner is a blemish on the television camera. Black and white specks are noise spikes in the data transmission.

9

THE ACCESSIBLE PARANORMAL AND THE NEW PSYCHOLOGY

> The borders of our minds are ever shifting
> And many minds can flow into one another . . .
> And create or reveal a single mind, a single energy.
>
> —W. B. Yeats

February 1987 started out as a low point in my life. My attempts to obtain civilian space contracts for my company failed. Space weapons work opportunities were abundant but I wasn't interested. There being no further work for me in my area of interest, it was becoming clear to me and to the management of my company that I had to leave. I started a long free fall into an uncertain future.

There was no woman in my life at the time and I wasn't even dating. I was finishing the manuscript for my last book, *Mars 1999*, in an intensely moody state.

On Friday February 13, I attended a meeting of the National Speakers Association in order to begin to make contacts in my newly chosen profession and focus—public speaking. I was tired, irritable and feeling sorry for myself as I walked into the reception room. There I met Laurene Johnson, who was later to become my significant other.

Even though I enjoyed our initial conversation and felt a special connection with her, I was overwhelmed with the need to sleep. I went home (which was in California at the time) totally exhausted, intensely worried about my future and feeling lonely. By all rights, when my head hit the pillow, I should have had a night of dreaming about my problems, tossing and turning my way into another depressing day.

Much to my surprise just the opposite happened. I dreamed I was lying in bed in a large high-ceiling room in Florence, Italy. The walls were pastel blue, with a crack in the plaster in the ceiling. I felt a rush of energy in my mid-forehead. This is sometimes called the third eye, one of the seven major chakra (energy) centers of the body first described in the traditional yogic literature and more recently rediscovered in Western transpersonal and "new age" theory and practice.

Then, as the connection between my third eye and the crack in the wall became almost laserlike, I experienced myself moving through this third eye out toward the crack, floating up near the top of the room. Not believing this could be real, I jerked back into my body lying in the bed. I was still aware of the dream room in Florence but now I also noticed the sounds of "real life" in my California beach apartment—the roar of the surf and the bell buoy. I realized this dream was probably lucid—taking place in normal self-reflective consciousness yet while dreaming in full color in what seemed to be Florence, but with the sounds coming into where I knew my physical body to be.

Once again I focused my energy through my third eye onto the crack on the wall in the hopes of traveling outside of my body again. Once more, I moved through and up to the crack, and then through it again and up into an attic, rapidly beneath the wood rafters, and then through the wall into the outside daylight, rising over Florence. The city was vivid and beautiful with its bright colored roofs and cathedrals. As I flew overhead I still noticed myself hearing the California surf and bell buoy. The scene then moved mysteriously to a Tudor house in England, which I floated around and inside for awhile.

I woke up euphoric, renewed and refreshed, and ready to tackle the day, even though it was six in the morning. What had happened? Why was I was able to embody so much energy during a time in which I should have felt terrible? Why Florence and England, places I had only visited briefly? I had never had an out-of-body experience. I didn't even know if they were possible. And I still am unclear about the incident, as I did not float above my California body; it was instead my body in my lucid dream. The experience appeared to superimpose qualities of both a lucid dream and an out-of-body experience. That whole next day I wrote, tackled my problems with confidence and poise, and joined Laurene for several hours of surprisingly pleasant conversation. Was there a connection between my dream and meeting Laurene? I believe there was.

I may have dismissed the experience as just another dream, albeit a lucid one, or an exhibition of vivid imagination, if it weren't for another incident regarding Laurene. Last summer we had broken up because of some seemingly irreconcilable emotional issues. We had been apart for months and it looked as though we would remain so, as we had agreed not to communicate. At 2:30 p.m. on August 26, 1988, I settled in my room to begin a prolonged meditation. At about seven that evening, in the midst of my meditation exercises, I was thinking about Laurene. My meditation deepened and I decided to break it for a moment to turn off my phone so I wouldn't be disturbed. Just as I was about to do this, it rang. It was Laurene. She was ill, she told me, and needed help. None of her friends were home and she was alone. She told me that at exactly 2:30 she had suddenly turned ill because of an abscessed tooth. Being the only one around to help, I drove over to her house to comfort her and we established an entirely new, more solid relationship.

The week prior to this chance reunion, we both had had several premonitions about our encounter. I had run into a friend of hers in San Diego and found myself intensely grieving again for the first time in two months about our breakup. And two nights prior, I had had a dream in which I sat at a table with Laurene and my mother while Laurene and I looked at each other confidently while holding hands under the table. This was the first time in months that I recalled Laurene being in a dream of mine.

Comparing notes, we both decided that our meeting was choreographed by some sort of cosmic energy that transcended mere chance and conscious cause and effect behavior. It seemed to be what Carl Jung called sychronicity, or acausal connectedness. Somehow, these encounters, dreams, thoughts and actions seemed designed to bring us together in a most dramatic encounter that was to determine our fates for years to come. The phenomena appeared to be directed by some higher power, while we merely seemed to blunder through life doing what we needed to do to handle situations as they came up.

This set of events that united and reunited Laurene and me were just one example of a string of paranormal experiences I was to have. I was later to learn that the paranormal might have been for me the fulfillment of the "show me" stage we former mainstream scientists must go through to turn from the world of superficial, tinker-toy mechanics to the more serious and mature world of loving spirituality and oneness with the universe. It was not the fact that I guessed the occupation of a stranger at a workshop that counted, or that I hiked the Grand Tetons in half the usual time, or that I was able to dream lucidly and seem to move out of my body. What seemed more important to me at the time was the feeling of joy and cosmic unity that accompanied these experiences. My own transformation temporarily superseded my desire to share and objectify my experience as a scientist, but this is the truth of the new reality—that it is an experienced reality, not an experiment or test. It is our life.

Relevance of the Paranormal

The mysterious, apparently transcendent panoply of experiences and experiments that seem to defy currently accepted laws of science is sometimes called the paranormal. Central to these phenomena are the new-reality principles that our inner space and outer space profoundly interact and that we create our own reality.

Having paranormal experiences is a more widespread activity than we might expect. According to a survey at the National Opinions Research Council and presented by sociologist Andrew Greeley, two-thirds of Americans report having had psychic experiences such as extrasensory perception. "What was paranormal is now normal," said Greeley. "It's even happening to elite scientists and physicians who insist that such things cannot possibly happen."

Research on the full range of paranormal experiences is too widespread to review adequately in this book. The first two meetings of the International Conferences on Paranormal Research held in 1988 and 1989 at Colorado State University, the books and bulletins issued by the Institute of Noetic Sciences, founded by fellow astronaut Edgar Mitchell, the formation of the Center for Studies in Science and Spirituality at the California Institute of Integral Studies, the continuing interest and support of metaphysical churches such as Religious Science and Unity, and the unexpectedly comprehensive and positive treatment by Time-Life Books in the *Mysteries of the Unknown* series, are all manifestations of recent interest in the subject. Research in this area has also been undertaken in the past by both the Parapsychological Association and the American Society for Psychical Research. Paranormal phenomena include extrasensory perception (ESP), psychokinesis, group experiences, precognition, channeling of nonphysical entities, out-of-body experiences, near death experiences, evidence for survival of physical death, spirit possession, and reincarnation. We have already dealt with two aspects of ESP in Backster's laboratory and in my reconnection with Laurene. In the rest of the chapter, we will look at the other phenomena I have listed, that fall within the general category of the paranormal.

Psychokinesis

Psychokinesis refers to the mind-over-matter capacity to lift, bend, transmute, or move materials simply by focusing one's energy or intention on them. There have been many documented examples of this phenomenon, including reports of gurus transporting themselves instantaneously from place to place (see *Life and Teaching of the Masters of the Far East* by Baird Spaulding). The materializations of the Indian guru Sai Baba, the widely-publicized spoon-bending by Uri Geller and others, and the mystery of how the earlier-mentioned ancient stone megaliths may have been transported, are other candidates for explanations that involve psychokinesis.

I have recently discovered that my speculations on megalithic stone levitation are consistent with a well-documented ceremony, held nowadays in the village of Shivapur near Poona in central India, and described in Francis Hitching's book *Earth Magic*. Eleven men in a circle surrounding a sacred stone are said to dance and chant for a few minutes and then cause it to levitate to shoulder level simply by touching it. "Many tourists have tried it successfully," according to Hitching.

Group Experiences

Communication among people appears to raise the collective energy and align the members of the group. I have had this experience many times in workshops such as Lifespring, Insight, and at spiritual events. One well-known demonstration of such a group experience is a "human wave" at a sporting event. I experienced a particularly dramatic example of this at the soccer final between France and Brazil held in the Rose Bowl at the 1984 Los Angeles Olympics. With over 100,000 participants, the stadium crowd at first appeared to me to be chaotic. People were unfriendly and restless as so often happens in crowds. Then a human wave began. I was amazed to find that not only did everybody in my vicinity participate, but the wave formed a distinct ribbon which slowly and uniformly propagated around the stadium. From the point of view of a physicist familiar with the properties of waves, this demonstration was fascinating because of the near-perfection of the wave form. Everybody seemed to know just when to stand up and applaud. As it ended, there appeared to be a feeling of exhilaration among many of us. Total strangers had somehow become connected by the energy passing through them.

These group experiences are consistent with the Gaia hypothesis described in Chapter 7. The entire planet may be a superorganism in which we humans are like cells consciously and unconsciously cooperating and competing. Such an analogy may connect us to Earth more than the notion that we are mere fleas on an elephant and are just beginning to be aware that the elephant is alive. In his well-written book, *The Global Brain*, Peter Russell proposes that we may sooner or later take an evolutionary leap to planetary consciousness.

Precognition

In *The Iceland Papers*, the French physicist Costa de Beauregard argues that quantum theory contains a time symmetry that allows for precognition, the ability to predict or determine the future. This bizarre trait is well-known among psychics, but there are some spectacular documented cases.

One such case comes from the parapsychologist Jule Eisenbud. In a 1972 interview with Richard Grossinger, Eisenbud discussed the ostensible ability of the Dutch psychic Bernard Croisset to predict the future. According to Eisenbud, "Croisset can pinpoint (the future) in a very specific and remarkable way and he's done this for over twenty years in his very extraordinary chair tests. He will put down statements about people who, two or three weeks later, on a given specified date, will occupy a space. And his statements will be correct, within certain limits, but certainly far beyond chance expectations. For instance, in the experiment we did, he was in Holland; on January 6, he said, some man who will take the ticket (you know, with a certain number; the ticket-dispensing thing was randomized) will be a man 5 feet 9½ inches tall, who works both in science and industry, who has a gold tooth in his lower jaw, who has something wrong with his big toe, a mark or scar, who has something to do with roulette, who lives in a house where someone plays the record player so loud that it's a nuisance and he can't stand it, and so on, and about half a dozen more statements, each of which were true. The man wandered in that night; he had never heard of Croisset in his life; he was a physicist, who took the ticket for this specific hot seat; he was a physicist for Dow Chemical, which is both science and industry; he was 5 feet 9 3/4; he's the only physicist there in a department of 11 physicists with a gold tooth in his lower jaw, who wears a steel plate because of bad surgery on an ingrown toenail; this was the 23rd of January; the statements were made on the 6th of January in Holland; who on the 19th of January drew a picture of intraatomic forces in his notebook, which looked just like a roulette wheel; and his particular hobby, this one was the change from the active to the passive, it isn't somebody in his house who plays the record-player too loud and continuously, he does, because he's addicted to bagpipe music; he turns it up as loud as he can, and the people at home can't stand it; it drives them up the walls. . . . To me, this type of thing, the ability to simply step over time, as if there were no barrier at all, is of such metaphysical, philosophical importance as to render everything else patent pending actually, until you understand. Everything else is almost trivial until you begin to understand what the hell goes on to enable a person to do this. All the work of physics stops at this point, and in fact, because of this physics, in its present form, is through . . .

"I have a theory here. You see, I don't think Croisset foretells the future; I think he creates it. He draws his people; you see, he scans the community for people with certain characteristics; he draws them there; he is able to control the shuffle; there is such a thing, you know, as a psychic shuffle . . ."

Channeling

Although having existed by other names in virtually all cultures and times, channeling has enjoyed a recent resurgence of interest and practice. It is a process that requires openness of a person to communication from an entity or presence of paranormal origin. According to Jon Klimo, a leading authority on the phenomenon and author of *Channeling: Investigations on Receiving Information from Paranormal Sources*, "Channeling is the communication of information to or through a physically embodied human being from a source that is said to exist on some other level or dimension of reality than the physical as we know it, and that is not from the normal mind (or self) of the channel." Such channeled presences or beings are often reported to possess an awareness about the past or future, or about other places in the universe beyond Earth, even in dimensions superior to ours. I have gone to several channels and been impressed by things I was told about myself and about the future that they couldn't have possibly known by to any normal means. While none of them has been 100% accurate, the best have been correct more than half the time. Especially impressive was their knowledge of some of the specifics of my life that they couldn't have known in any way other than paranormally. For example, the invisible source speaking through one channel went on cheerily about my special interest in international missions to Mars as well as specific aspects of a personal relationship. It was highly unlikely I was known to her, as I had walked into her office as a stranger to her; but I can never know this for certain.

Out of Body Experiences

One of the richest descriptions of out-of-body experience (OBE) is in Virginia businessman Robert Monroe's book, *Journeys Out of the Body*. In order to try to make sense of his experience and to help others who where having OBEs, he wrote his book and later founded an institute devoted to studying and teaching about this curious phenomenon. He developed brain-hemisphere synchronization sound tapes to induce an altered state of consciousness conducive to having out of body experiences. Visitors to the Monroe Institute have the opportunity to feel the sensations of their consciousness moving up and out of their bodies and floating into other rooms and even into distant cities, like my earlier lucid dream about Florence.

Researchers have not conclusively determined whether the OBE is a paranormal experience involving a "second body" or "astral projection" that travels away from the physical body, whether it is a form of ESP, or whether it is simply a manifestation of an altered state that draws on the imagination. Parapsychologist Charles Tart, in his introduction to Monroe's book, came to these conclusions about OBEs based on his own research: OBEs are widespread across cultures and time and are generally experienced once in a lifetime, they are usually one of the most profound and joyful experiences of a person's life, and, in some instances, "the description of what was happening at a distant place is correct and more accurate than we would expect by coincidence. . . . To explain these we must postulate either that the 'hallucinatory' experience of the OBE was combined with the operation of ESP, or that in some sense the person really was 'there'. The OBE then becomes very real indeed."

Near Death Experience

Individuals who have nearly died and come back report having had experiences similar to out of body ones. Many books have been written about the paranormal events that seem to accompany death or near death. These events include feelings of peace and well-being, separating from the body, entering darkness or a tunnel, seeing a light, entering that light, and then a whole set of possibilities such as a life review, meeting deceased loved ones, and deciding to come back to continue life here, usually with less fear of death and a revitalized joy for life as a result. The only exception is revived suicides, who report a sort of hell, which tends to confirm the Tibetan belief that we create our own reality even after death, thus the frame of mind in which we die is important. According to a 1982 Gallup poll, 8 million Americans have reported having had the near death experience.

When not yet aware of this phenomenon, I myself had a near death experience. In March 1982 I was driving alone from New York to Boston. It had been raining, a cold front had moved in, and the road suddenly became icy. Going sixty miles an hour, I skidded. My car overturned many times, crashed off guard rails and into a deep ditch. It was wrecked like an accordion, with the only remaining space inside being that which contained my body.

I emerged from the accident completely unhurt. A professional automobile insurance adjuster who had witnessed the accident and run up to the car expecting to find one or more corpses, was astounded at the sight of my healthy body. He stood at my window asking incredulously, "Are you all right?"

"I'm fine," I said, quietly walking away from the wreck.

Actually I felt euphoric but shocked. I had remembered that when the car began to skid out of control, all feeling left my body. I heard dull thuds and felt as if I were freely floating above the accident, moving in almost timeless slow motion. I remember darkness and some bobbing bright lights and then an awesome peaceful silence.

The accident report revealed an almost incredibly improbable survival. How I wasn't even injured still amazes me. But it served at least one essential purpose: I began to move to change my life and increasingly to accept the new reality. I sensed that I needed to be in an environment that nurtured and encouraged my inner-space development. Within one month, I bought a used Ford van, packed all my possessions, and moved to California. The accident and the accompanying near-death experience were needed to shake me into a move. I felt as though I had some sort of guardian angel charged with keeping me on this planet, at least for awhile longer.

Hypnotic Regression, Past Lives and Reincarnation

When I arrived in California in the spring of 1982, I felt I needed to find out more about death and survival, and so I began a series of metaphysical adventures that far exceeded what I had bargained for back in Philadelphia in 1977. I even began to have some hypnotic regressions to alleged former lives.

My first recall under hypnosis was of having been given a death summons in a jail cell in what appeared to be the Vatican. Somehow I felt I had done or said something the church didn't like. I was very shaky about the summons, as it sealed my fate. When the hypnotist asked me how I died, I saw myself tied to a stake in a courtyard, being stoned or burned. The recollection was too traumatic as I moved up out of my body and over the courtyard and viewed the execution from above. All this imagery was involuntary and took place before I even knew about the out of the body process, let alone about how this could be done to avoid the pain of trauma.

I wondered if this was really a past life recall or just a dream or a fantasy. Was the fact that I was raised Catholic in this lifetime sublimated in the dream? Or, was my guilt about having negative thoughts as a child, and my almost overwhelming desire as an adult to have all of us transform ourselves from political, religious, and scientific orthodoxy, just a continuation of this unsatisfactory resolution of a former life? By far the most exciting evidence for reincarnation is found in the research of Dr. Ian Stevenson at the University of Virginia. In interviewing children younger than six years of age, Stevenson uncovered vivid recalls of past lives. His research in over 1600 cases worldwide was meticulous and carefully controlled to avoid fraud, or instances potentially explicable by ESP, possession, etc. He concluded that in many cases at least some aspect of the human personality leaves the physical body that has died and later reenters another body, usually within a few years. His results also suggest that the spirit may actually choose its parents for the next life.

I was heartened to feel that we had a scientific basis for the survival of death and for recycling back to the planet, and yet I felt a nagging discomfort that something was wrong. I didn't quite want to let go of years of investment in either Catholic doctrine or reductionistic science. I needed to find new inner experiences to remove these doubts. I was like a child clinging to Santa Claus —the kind of sterile, giftless Santa Claus adults create to give them the illusion of power. I still preferred the trivial control over minor experimental results of science to the heart-warming lack of control we have in a far vaster, more designed universe.

Ketamine

On one occasion I decided to take a psychic voyage of discovery into the possibility of other dimensions of human experience. Not knowing anything specific about what would happen, I chose under medical supervision to receive a mind-altering medication called ketamine or vitamin K. I did not want to prejudice my experience with expectations or wishful thinking. What I did know was that Ketamine is sometimes used as an anesthesia for cats. It induces unconsciousness for only twenty to forty minutes and is not psychoactive like LSD. The well-known dolphin researcher and maverick scientist John Lilly used it frequently to explore his own consciousness and the other dimensions of reality that such altered states apparently allowed him to enter. I was supervised by trusted professionals who assured me that the experience would be safe.

As I went under I felt a blacking out and only an awareness of the roof of my mouth. In my mind, as I went deeper, I addressed my fears about its effects. Will I come out of this? Am I physically dead? Is this also spiritual suicide? I found myself repeating the name of my supervisor many times in echo-like fashion. Then I began to explore territory of which I had never been previously aware.

What happened next truly amazed me. I saw myself not in human form but simply being. I found myself moving rapidly through a three-dimensional tapestry of the richest colors and textures I had ever seen. If Disney Productions had a trillion-dollar budget it could not have matched the experience I was having. Geometric forms, mountains and valleys, transforming shapes and semi-living beings swung by me. I also had a license to expand on what was being presented to me by performing my own zoom sequences and by transforming images at will.

My exact thoughts are hard to recollect. One of them, however, was that perhaps I was dead and, if so, this was nonetheless acceptable. I recall having felt that life on Earth was but a small part of my total reality. I looked upon my mundane problems of money, career, and relationships with a sense of benign detachment and overview. My problems, even the prospects for the rest of life, receded to tiny proportions. I felt at one with something so much larger that it is impossible to describe. The only physical metaphor for understanding where I was going was the enormity of space experienced by the astronomer and astronaut. Our Milky Way galaxy contains one hundred billion stars, and we have billions of more galaxies accessible to our telescopes. We Earthlings certainly are insignificant in the sheer vastness of our inner *and* outer space; our significance therefore must lie in our ability to observe and reflect its complexity and delicate structure.

What surprised me most in the Ketamine-induced experience was that I could somehow relate intimately to much of what was happening. The rich imagery presented to me seemed remarkably human in the sense that I could see, remember, experience and describe it. It was not esoteric or intangible. It was very real. During most of the experience my only Earthly cues were those of hearing a dog barking and of sensing the roof of my mouth. These physical awarenesses had small but anchoring impact compared to my exotic journey; it was as if only a token part of me remained on our planet. If the building I was in were to catch fire, I don't think I could have responded: I was too far out of the physical dimensions.

Perhaps nobody is more in touch with the Ketamine experience than John Lilly, who wrote about this in his revealing autobiography *The Scientist.* Lilly has taken Ketamine thousands of times, and he admits this occasionally affected his health and loosened his connection to what he called the consensus reality on Earth. He had many of these experiences in a human isolation tank, unaffected by gravity, light and sound.

When he took doses comparable to mine, Lilly described his experience as follows (in the third person): "If he closed his eyes he saw continuous motion-picture-like sequences, highly colored, three-dimensional, and consisting of, at first, inanimate scenes which later became populated with various strange and unusual creatures as well as human beings . . . His relationship to his physical body became weakened and attenuated. He found that he began to participate in scenes which were previously merely visual images, as if it were there, outside of his body . . ."

Shifting to writing in the first person, Lilly continued: "I have left my body floating in a tank on the planet Earth. This is a very strange and alien environment. It must be extraterrestrial, I have not been here before. I must be on some other planet in some civilization other than the one in which I was evolved. I am in a peculiar state of high indifference. I am not involved in either fear or love. I am a highly neutral being, watching and waiting."

He then described seeing brilliant creatures moving around a strange purple planet attempting to send thoughts to him. He calls these experiences "the extraterrestrial reality," while he calls the rapidly moving colors that he first saw "the internal reality." Evidently I was straddling the two with my moderate dose. Is it possible that the mere act of inducing altered states of consciousness with regard to our *inner space* can create the extraordinarily real experience of movement at will through space, time, and other dimensions, just as our alleged UFO visitors appear to be able to operate with regard to *outer space*? Will outer space travel become easier once we realize that the farthest reaches of all space may be visited through our inner space?

But Lilly's travels took him much further. With larger doses of Ketamine, he found a threshold in which the "I" disappeared. He saw himself tapping into a network of creation, of a mind at one with all the making of all universes. And at even larger doses, he found himself entering an indescribable void which he called The Unknown.

This voyage might be likened to falling into a black hole in outer space, or perhaps going back to the hypothesized primordial mass of creation prior to the Big Bang. These are spaces and times, so to speak, in which there is no space or time as we know them, only an altered set of laws of physics beyond our comprehension. Had Lilly entered this forbidden territory? Perhaps so. Could we all? Again, perhaps. I wonder if all of astronomy, astrophysics, and related science is not a protective decoy to keep us out of the "real" universe until we are ready.

Demons, Spirit Possession, Ghosts, and Psychic Manipulation

Several years ago, I was lying alone in bed unclothed during a period of depression in my life. Expressing privately to myself my deepest despair, I suddenly perceived a strange man on the roof outside my window heckling and ridiculing me. In two years I had never seen a person on that roof. It was inaccessible to pedestrians unless someone had a ladder and were making a repair. I don't have any further memories of this incident, whose darkness I have tried hard to forget. I was literally caught with my pants down in my lowest consciousness, the possible fulfillment of the negative effects of putting out negative energy. Was this a demon of my own making?

I was also once in a table-tipping seance with a medium who summoned allegedly deceased spirits who may have been troubled or malevolent. The experience seemed to drain our energies. I was so tired I went to sleep for ten hours and missed an important business meeting that next morning.

The possession of humans by deceased spirits has been widely reported throughout time. According to the theory of possession, the "spirits" or "souls" of some persons who die (usually from sudden or tragic causes) become confused and, rather than ascending to the "light" or the higher levels of consciousness, they attach themselves to spiritually unprotected living people on Earth. For example, it could happen to a person who is drunk, or who is under anesthesia in the hospital. These people then become "possessed" and are often drained of their energies. For centuries, Catholic priests, Tibetan shamans, and others have performed exorcisms to eject these attached spirits. This procedure has been brought up-to-date by psychiatrists and psychologists who hypnotise their subjects and "talk" the spirit into leaving the bodies of those to which they are attached. While all this might sound like science fiction, the cures using this procedure can be dramatic and instantaneous. In the book *The Unquiet Dead* by Edith Fiore and in several papers presented at the Second International Conference on Paranormal Research at Colorado State University in June, 1989, the issues in spirit depossession therapy are discussed.

Our movie industry and the tabloids have made profitable use of human encounters with spirit attachments, ghosts and demons, as well as poltergeists, UFO abductions, and other mysterious happenings on the dark side. These spectacular examples, along with the more common occurrence of psychic manipulations by disembodied spirits and would-be healers, provide ample warning that not all our explorations of inner space are filled with a euphoric sense of awe, or a breakthrough into higher consciousness.

I have had experiences with individuals who have identified themselves as healers but have also presented a dark side. Without being too specific, so as to protect the anonymity of those individuals, I have been able to identify a pattern of their activities. First they build up your ego so you feel you're somebody very special. Then they encourage you to participate in various healing sessions, closed-eye processes, and workshops under their charismatic leadership, and they demonstrate to you some of their psychic insights and powers. After that, when you are brought under their influence, they appear as self-appointed gurus who devise processes that encourage you to change your life direction (for example, in career and relationships). This kind of psychic manipulation can be subtle at first but later could be devastating to an unsuspecting individual. I believe much of this manipulative behavior is a power trip, analogous to a dictator of a nation beginning to assert his authority. Advocates of any reality, old or new, can include in its ranks charlatans as well as enlightened beings.

Many groups such as the fundamentalist Christian churches are acutely aware of the dangers of becoming subject to the psychic manipulations from occult sources, and they admonish their parishioners to stay away from these things. I believe they have a point: we all know about the powerful influences of cults, of which the Symbionese Liberation Army and Jim Jones' Guyana commune are primary examples. The problem is, many of these church groups carry their critique so far as to eliminate consideration of the entire range of the paranormal and metaphysical. In this way, the churches are behaving much like those mainstream scientists who oppose virtually all aspects of the new reality. The main difference between the evangelists and the scientists is that the former fear the very real influence of the occult, whereas the latter fear the anti-rational destruction of their familiar models. But both groups seem to be fervent in hoping the new reality will go away, as attested by numerous articles and books written by both the conservative church members and the scientific skeptics.

Search for a New Psychological Model

The full range of the paranormal absolutely requires for its understanding an emerging conceptual framework in the form of a new psychology: what is the human mind (including holographic and energetic aspects) and how does it function? Does it survive death? We will need to abandon the old reductionistic models of our minds being contained within a computer-like brain that acts as a control center with specialized modular units that run each of our separated bodies as if we were robots. Any model building on behalf of a new psychology must explore how our minds are apparently interconnected with one another's and with the realities of both physical and non-physical realms in ways that appear to have been demonstrated by recent research. Such a model must also explore our immortality, or at least the possibility that our consciousness can operate separate from our physical bodies. If it is the task of psychologists to address the mind, they will need to look at what both the mystics and new scientists have been saying about it and depart from their simplistic models and metaphors of perception and learning.

What we do know is that our minds appear to influence matter, and this suggests that we reverse the hierarchy of our sciences. Rather than focusing on physics to explain the ultimate properties of our universe we must look first at the spiritual, holistic, and mind sciences, then the biological sciences, chemistry, and physics.

This new primacy of mind over matter, of spirit over the material, is called "downward causation" by Nobel laureate Roger Sperry and by scientist-futurist Willis Harman. In other words, it is no longer sufficient to understand how things work simply by looking at the behaviors of the smallest particles. When these particles unite to form a reality greater than the sum of their parts (atoms, molecules, cells, humans, planets, universes, etc.), the whole system takes on unique characteristics. "The concepts of physical reality," said Sperry, "and the kind of cosmology upheld by science in the two conflicting views differ vastly, particularly with respect to their psychological and humanistic implications."

Holograms and Extremely Low Frequency Waves

One model of the brain/mind which begins to satisfy experimental results is that of the hologram. First proposed by the Stanford neuroscientist Karl Pribram, this looks at the brain as a processor of frequencies rather than of images. Each portion of the brain also contains information about the whole rather than a specialized fragment. "Our brains mathematically construct 'concrete reality'," says author Marilyn Ferguson, "by interpreting frequencies from our new dimension, a realm of meaningful, patterned primary reality that transcends time and space. The brain is a hologram interpreting a holographic universe.

"The holographic model", she continues, "resolves one long-standing riddle of (psychic phenomena): the inability of instrumentation to track the apparent energy transfer in telepathy, healing, clairvoyance. If those events occur in a dimension transcending time and space, there is no need for energy to travel from here to there. As one researcher put it, 'There isn't any *there!*'"

The artist William de Kooning continues to paint masterpieces even though he suffers from Alzheimer's Disease to a degree that he cannot recognize friends and family. Who is doing the painting?

This model is also consistent with University of London theoretical physicist David Bohm's version of the new physics. "Relativity" he said, "and, even more important, quantum mechanics have strongly suggested (though not proved) that the world cannot be analyzed into separate and independently existing parts. Moreover, each part somehow involves all the others: contains them or enfolds them. This fact suggests that the sphere of ordinary material life and the sphere of mystical experience have a certain shared order and that this will allow a fruitful relationship between them."

As interestingly as this model may seem to apply to our new view of science, several leading writers such as transpersonal psychology pioneer Ken Wilbur and Willis Harman warn that the essence of our emerging new science must transcend the hologram. A hologram is static, for example, whereas consciousness is active. Consciousness might be better described as a cause, thus might give rise to a hologram, rather than be one.

A second model for explaining the paranormal involves extremely low frequency (ELF) waves from weak magnetic fields that are apparently self-organizing and operate at the sub-quantum level. The American physician Andrija Puharich has proposed that these waves constitute a fifth force of nature, separate from electromagnetic waves, which could explain the full range of paranormal and healing phenomena. Unlike electromagnetic waves, these waves do not weaken with the inverse square of the distance. According to Puharich, they penetrate all materials except for the DNA molecule, which can be transmuted by sending the waves at appropriate frequencies, such as from a psychic healer. A frequency of eight cycles per second (or eight Hertz) can produce a healing reaction, but a frequency of seven cycles per second can be destructive; for example, in spoon-bending. Puharich has measured these frequencies with electroencephalographic (EEG) brainwave FM broadcasts and ELF detectors in connection with transformation caused by healers such as the Brazilian psychic surgeon Arigo and with metal benders such as Uri Geller. He also laments the ELF "psychic warfare" which has apparently been taking place in secret between the United States and the Soviet Union, involving efforts to "irradiate" the psyches of citizens of the other nation.

Physicist Bob Beck has also studied the brain wave patterns of healers throughout the world and found them all to emit these seven to eight Hertz waves while in their altered states regardless of their cultural background and healing modality. Interestingly, he discovered that these waves were both frequency- and phase-synchronized with the observed Schumann waves of the Earth—

oscillations in the Earth's magnetic and electric fields. These measurements led John Zimmerman, founder of the Bio-Electromagnetics Institute in Boulder, Colorado, to propose a theory in which healers "tune into" the Earth's Schumann waves and achieve "coherence" with their own brain waves and biomagnetic fields, which in turn match the brain waves of the patient. This theory could be tested in space, well beyond the effects of the Schumann waves of the Earth, to see if the healings might still be effective. Perhaps we have once again the interaction between human and Earth energies. If Puharich, Beck and Zimmerman are right, we are becoming aware of a powerful and effective tool which would revolutionize all the sciences.

Models of Other Realms

In the end, we will need to employ more than holograms and psychic waves to explain the new reality. If we do indeed survive life and reincarnate, we will need to investigate the possible existence of other realms of our being beyond the physical. Existing models come from age-old, mystical traditions, the teachings of contemporary spiritual leaders such as John-Roger, the channeling process, contacts with alleged extraterrestrials, and the developing research literature (by Maurice Albertson and Kenneth Freeman, for example) that explores the paranormal in earnest.

According to the inner space astronauts, some of these realms are nonphysical and remain mostly unacknowledged. The next higher realm above the physical is sometimes called the astral, which is most accessible to us in the form of our imaginations, out-of-body experiences, and our lifting out of our physical bodies in dreams and perhaps after death. Higher still are said to be the causal and mental planes that move us through the cause-and-effect of our lessons and provide the basis for operating as one mind. Yet another realm either above the astral, causal and mental or between the physical and astral, has been identified as the etheric plane, which appears to be a vast void, the unknown of the unconscious forces that sometimes mysteriously drive us. This is where much of the apparent magic of the paranormal events takes place, the realm of the masters of the Far East. And above all these is the soul realm, a level of evolution of the soul that requires no more reincarnation and involves an ecstatic oneness with the universe.

The Inner Space Astronaut

For all the times I have had paranormal experiences or may have recalled other lives and realms I am sure I have missed many other opportunities because of the limitations of my five senses, my own skepticism, my chattering censoring mind, human language, and all the other things that trap us here within our everyday existences. We have seen that the scientific skeptics tend to armor themselves with mundane explanations of the paranormal to protect their own professional paradigm. Therefore, they see nothing new. But our minds await a transformation to being able to experience more and more paranormal events . . . if only we can open ourselves to our fullest potential to accept them as integral parts of our reality.

If we refuse to do it ourselves, it will be imposed on us, or at least on some of us. This certainly has been true for me at those times I have been in my lowest, as well as my and highest, consciousness. For the most part, I cannot as yet summon the paranormal at will. This is true of most of us: paranormal encounters apparently come to us spontaneously, as when we encounter a UFO, we have a near-death experience, or when 70,000 people witness the sun spinning at Fatima. For some of us, there are a few exceptions to this kind of spontaneity; for example, the paranormal seems to regularly occur when the children of Medjugorje, Yugoslavia, talk to a visiting other-dimensional Queen of Peace delivering urgent messages to humankind; when a master repeatedly materializes and dematerializes; when someone experiments with consciousness-altering substances, machines, or meditative practices; or when the minds of tens of thousands of ordinary people are convinced that they can walk painlessly over hot coals and do it successfully against all physical odds.

Clearly, I have had to suspend disbelief and make a metaphysical plunge. As philosopher Sam Keen put it, "The goal of self-exploration is beyond our wildest imagination but at least the first steps on the path are clear. The journey into the cosmic-evolutionary dimensions of the self cannot begin until we have dared go beneath the images of self given us by our parents and our peers. The first step is to break out of the persona, the character armor created by our 'normal' process of psychological development. We must go beyond the threshold which is guarded by *guilt* and *shame* (the guardians of conscience which represent the values and visions of the Giants—Parents and Authorities). . . . It is only when we have passed through this theater of the multiplicity of the roles of the self (the killer, the playboy, the victim, the saint, etc.) that we may pass beyond the second threshold to where the journey into cosmic-evolutionary dimensions of the self begins. And that adventure is endless."

I have become an astronaut of inner space. During the 1980s I have been driven from within to sample a smorgasbord of activities and practices that would have taken a lifetime of systematic research to achieve while maintaining a sense of continuity, caution, and discernment. I have taken dozens of workshops, gone on retreats, read books, listened to tapes, seen therapists, chiropractors, acupuncturists, jin shin therapists, aura balancers, polarity balancers, yoga teachers, rebirthers, medicine men, psychics, channelers, astrologers, and Tarot card readers. I have chanted in groups and alone, have meditated for periods from minutes to hours to days. I have worked with crystals, lain down in sensory deprivation tanks and attached machines to my head and body to assist in altering my consciousness. I have visited and dowsed at many of the planet's sacred sites. And I became a minister in the Movement of Spiritual Inner Awareness, a loosely knit spiritual organization dedicated to transcending the self into a soul "I am" awareness.

The array of possible experiences one can undertake is almost endless and it is easy to go down the wrong path. Just as exploring outer space requires checking your coordinates and your motion so that you reach your destination safely, the inner journey requires discernment in picking out the most prudent paths. And, from the testimonies of the mystics, sooner or later we will need to let go of the exciting paranormal feast, to fast, and to fall into our true selves. We must let go of the ego in order to enter the more inclusive "I am" as the true self. This process involves energies, dimensions, and awarenesses that we are only beginning to understand and use as a species.

The Perennial Philosophy and the Primordial Tradition

Psychology and the exploration of the inner spaces long associated with mind and spirit combine in what writer Aldous

Huxley called the "perennial philosophy." This basic truth pervades all of us as individuals and cuts across the arbitrary beliefs of the world's religions and sciences. It is, as Huxley put it, a wisdom which "recognizes a divine Reality substantial to the world of things and lives and minds; the psychology that finds something similar to, or even identical with, divine Reality; the ethic that places man's final end in the knowledge of the immanent and transcendent Ground of all being."

The Canadian theologian John Rossner refers to this cosmic perspective as the "primordial tradition" that also intersects all religions through all time. Rossner shared a unique voyage to India with astronaut Ed Mitchell, his wife Marilyn (a psychic), and the Indian swami Devananda, the group issued a joint statement to the lay audiences they addressed: "Up to this point in history of the West, we have adopted rational sciences and material techniques. And we have been busy exporting them to the peoples of India and the Third World. Now we are here to ask you by all means to continue to take our technologies and our sciences. . . . But please do not take along with them our reductionistic Western philosophical assumptions. For these unnecessarily limit human psychic and spiritual potential, and ultimately will lead science into a cul-de-sac. . . . India's ancient yogic insights could one day be used by individuals in both East and West in building new psi-cognizant sciences. With such future sciences mankind could one day rediscover transcendent worlds of 'inner space' . . ."

Marilyn Rossner expressed the problem of our Western tunnel-vision even more bluntly. "Only tangible demonstrations," she said, "of the reality of the human psychic facilities: ESP, PK, spiritual healing, and communication with the beloved departed in and through the Spirit of God, will ever break down the false materialistic models of reality that some modern scientists and philosophers have created . . . so many persons today oppose the exploration of psychic phenomena with a blind rage and denials without open-minded exploration."

Conclusion

Through exploring the reality of the paranormal, we come face to face with the fact that we are immortal cosmic beings as well as mortal Earthlings. For the first time in centuries and perhaps even millennia, we seem to have an opportunity to use this greater awareness to transcend the struggles of mankind and to live life more fully and joyfully. "Now a new and higher consciousness," writes philosopher Obadiah Harris, "is preparing for those who can receive and take advantage of its presence. On this rests the hope of the future and destiny of man. For all the difficulties will be laid on it and overcome which the man of mental consciousness has proven unable to master."

To embrace this higher consciousness, the new psychology must go beyond the laboratory data and analytical thinking that have been deemed acceptable. It must probe the mysterious as well as the already-understood aspects of the human mind. Research and our own personal experiences point to an extraordinary interdependence of minds with one another and with the universe and they mandate new perceptions far beyond the five senses.

But the paranormal is more a guidepost than a consumator. We still need to do the hard work of removing our physical, motional and mental blocks to self-transcendence and self-realization. We must first heal the estrangement that exists between our inner and outer spaces.

Bibliography

Albertson, Maurice L. and Kenneth P. Freeman, "Research Related to Reincarnation," *Paranormal Research*, Rocky Mountain Research Institute, Ft. Collins, Colo., p. 355 (1988).

Beck, Robert O., "Mood Modification with ELF Magnetic Fields: A Preliminary Exploration, *Archaeus*, Volume 4, p. 48 (1986).

Bohm, David, back cover in *The Holographic Paradigm*, edit. by Ken Wilber, New Science Library, Boston (1982).

Castenada, Carlos, *Tales of Power*, Simon and Schuster, New York (1974).

Eisenbud, Jule, interview, p. 164 in *Ecology and Consciousness*, edited by Richard Grossinger, North Atlantic Books, Berkeley, Calf. (1978).

Ferguson, Marilyn, pp. 22-23 in *The Holographic Paradigm*, edit. by Ken Wilber, New Science Library, Boston (1982).

Fiore, Edith, *The Unquiet Dead*, Ballentine, New York (1987).

Gallup, George Jr., *Adventures in Immortality*, McGraw-Hill, New York (1982).

Greeley, Andrew, "The Impossible: It's Happening," *American Health: Fitness of Body and Mind*, January-February 1987 and *Noetic Sciences Review*, Spring 1987.

Harman, Willis, "An Extended Science," *Noetic Sciences Review*, Summer and Fall 1987.

Harris, Obadiah, *The New Consciousness*, Pendell Publishing Company, Midland, Michigan, p. vii (1977).

Huxley, Aldous, *The Perennial Philosophy*, Harper & Row, New York (1970).

The Iceland Papers, edit. by Andrija Puharich, Essentia Research Associates, Amherst, Wisconsin (1979).

John-Roger, *Passage into Spirit*, Baraka, Los Angeles, (1984).

Keen, Sam, pp. 116-118 in *The Holographic Paradigm*, edit. by Ken Wilbur, New Science Library, Boston (1982).

Klimo, Jon, *Channeling: Investigations on Receiving Information from Paranormal Sources*, Tarcher, Los Angeles (1987).

Lilly, John C., *The Scientist*, Ronin, Berkeley (1988).

Monroe, Robert A., *Journeys Out of the Body*, Doubleday, New York (1971).

Mysteries of the Unknown, Time-Life book series, Alexandria, Virginia (1987).

Paranormal Research, edit. by Maurice L. Albertson, Dan S. Ward and Kenneth P. Freeman, Rocky Mountain Research Institute, Ft. Collins, Colo. (1988 and 1989).

Pribram, Karl H., pp. 27-34 in *The Holographic Paradigm*, edit. by Ken Wilbur, New Science Library, Boston (1982).

Puharich, Andrijah, "Magnetic Model of Matter and Mind Unifying the Five Forces of Nature," Temple University Conference on Frontier Issues in Physics, Biology and Quantum Theory, Bermuda, April 1988.

Ring, Kenneth, *Heading Toward Omega: In Search for Meaning of the Near Death Experience*, Morrow, New York (1984).

Roberts, Jane, *The Nature of Personal Reality*, Prentice-Hall, Englewood Cliffs, NJ (1974).

Rossner, John, *In Search of the Primordial Tradition and the Cosmic Christ*, p. xxv, The Llewellyn New Times, St. Paul, Minnesota (1989).

Rossner, Marilyn Zwaig, "God's Guidance and Natural Forms of Psychic Communication," a lecture reprinted by the Spiritual Science Fellowship, Montreal, September, 1978.

Russell, Peter, *The Global Brain*, Tarcher, Los Angeles (1983).

Spaulding, Baird T., *Life & Teaching of the Masters of the Far East*, De Vorrs, Marina del Rey, Calf. (1924).

Sperry, Roger, "Downward Causation," *The Journal of Mind and Behavior*, Winter 1987 and the *Noetic Sciences Review*, Fall 1987.

Stevenson, Ian, "Reincarnation: Field Studies and Theoretical Issues," *Handbook of Parapsychology*, edit by Benjamin B. Wolmer, Van Nostrand Reinhold, New York (1977).

Zimmerman, John, "Laying-on-of-Hands Healing and Therapeutic Touch: A Testable Theory," *Paranormal Research*, pp. 656-672, edit. by Maurice L. Albertson, Dan S. Ward and Kenneth P. Freeman, Rocky Mountain Research Institute, Ft. Collins, Colo. (1988).

10

HEALING OURSELVES AND OUR PLANET

> The whole purpose of science is to awaken the cosmic religious feeling.
>
> —Albert Einstein, *Ideas and Opinions*

In this chapter we shall see that the revolution in healing and health care that employs the mind, homeopathic medicines, and other unorthodox healing approaches is far outstripping the limitations of reductionistic medicine. When it comes to the power of the mind, we are forced to stand in awe and say that we don't yet know why or how such anomalous or "miraculous" healing works—we just know it works. And if it works, we should use it.

Time and again I have seen healings take place through the power of the mind. Although they may seem to violate materialistic, scientific and medical practice and all that we were trained to believe, they can literally change the chemistry of cells. The proof that such alternative modes of healing work is so extensive that we now have perhaps the greatest immediate benefit of our new reality. The transformation of our traditional medicine into a healing art based on the perennial philosophy, a transformation of now well under way, seems to embody the metaphor that we are using our innermost space to influence the "outer space" of our bodies.

My Own Healing

Last spring on a trip to Peru I jammed my right knee into the side of a seat as I was getting heavy luggage down from a rack on a train. I felt considerable pain at the time, and it seemed to feel worse rather than better after I got back home weeks later. I visited one of the best-known orthopedic sports- medicine doctors in the Southwest. She took my X-ray and gave me some bad news: my injury, she said, aggravated an already existing condition of "severe advanced arthritis." She went on to say that the knee had no cartilage and that I would need to have an operation, or else I would be wearing a brace and limping for the rest of my life. I was given no hope for any other form of healing.

After a day or two of feeling helpless, I decided I did not want to accept the diagnosis. Instead, I asserted to myself that, although the knee was injured, it would heal quickly with the appropriate loving care. I stopped taking the pain killers I had been given. I bathed the knee with "inner" light and touched it with care. I did this by closing my eyes, relaxing, breathing deeply and imagining a healing white light passing through my knee. I asked others to do this to me also. Soon I was walking normally and within one month I was hiking in the Colorado Rockies.

I revisited the doctor and told her all that had transpired. She stuck with her former diagnosis and guessed that I was temporarily feeling relief from a chronic condition. I didn't have a second X-ray taken, which would have been interesting for research purposes. I asked the doctor if she thought it was possible to heal with thoughts and loving only. Her pragmatic response was that if it works, why not do it.

One year later my knee is still fine. I hike and ski frequently. Although I cannot say that my healing unequivocally was mental or spiritual, I would be most surprised if it was not. If I can change the chemistry of a glass of water by blessing it, why could I not change the chemistry of my knee by blessing it? Fortunately, my claims of healing are borne out by the experiences of millions of people worldwide and practiced with reported success by people in such churches as Religious Science, Unity, and Christian Science.

Perhaps there is no better example of miraculous healings than that of Lourdes in France. "The careful work of the Lourdes Medical Bureau," Michael Murphy, founder of the Esalen Institute, points out, "has produced a huge share of case histories providing many insights on the body's remarkable responsiveness to spiritual influence. . . . Because the cures at Lourdes have been screened with such care and examined from so many points of view, there is overwhelming evidence that many of them are authentic. . . . These events seem to show that human beings universally possess supernormal capacities which begin to function once certain conditions of body and mind are established, whether their recipient anticipates them or not."

Murphy describes the positive effects that raising our consciousness can have on our bodies. "When we focus upon the *co*-evolution of form and consciousness, the body side of the equation is no longer seen to be inferior. . . . The regularity with which powers are released by transformative disciplines in every culture makes it conceivable that all of us harbor the same latent supernature."

The power of the mind within the healing process is well demonstrated by writer and former *Saturday Review* editor Norman Cousins. For decades he has been an articulate and outspoken advocate of transforming our present political systems to a peaceful world order. A few years ago, Cousins began to fall victim to a seemingly irreversible paralysis of his body. The doctors told Cousins he had one chance in 500 of recovery.

Cousins went for that one in 500 chance. He refused to accept a negative outcome and so decided to try to cure himself. While he approached the problem as an eager and curious (lay) scientist, he worked in particular to inject his illness with as much *humor* as possible. The end result was what was almost certainly a self-cure followed by much insight which he shared with the public regarding the impact of a positive attitude upon our health.

"Over the years," said Cousins, "medical science has identified the primary systems of the human body . . . But two other systems that are central to the proper functioning of a human being need to be emphasized: the healing system and the belief system. The two work together. The healing system is the way the body mobilizes all its resources to combat disease. The belief system is often the activator of the healing system.

"The belief system represents the unique element in human beings that makes it possible for the human mind to affect the workings of the body. How one responds—intellectually, emotionally, spiritually—to one's problems has a great deal to do with the way the human body functions. One's confidence, or lack of it, in the prospects of recovery from serious illness affects the chemistry of the body. The belief system converts hope, robust expectations and the will to live into plus factors in any contest of forces involving disease."

Homeopathic and Vibrational Medicine

About two months before this writing, I acquired an out-of-control cough I had never had before. It was both frightening and embarrassing to me—frightening because at times I had trouble catching my breath between successive coughs and embarrassing because it could happen at any time and any place including public appearances when people thought I might be choking to death.

I decided not to take any antibiotics for this condition, even though I realized they would probably relieve the symptoms immediately. I had just heard too many stories of the negative side effects of antibiotics, such as weakening the immune system and contracting diseases such as Candida and perhaps eventually cancer, diabetes, and heart disease.

I decided to go to a homeopathic doctor to treat my cough. This branch of medicine employs cures whose chemical composition is similar to that of the disease—analogous to immunization shots. What makes homeopathy mysterious in an orthodox scientific context is that these medicines often heal the body without any of the side effects of traditional medicines and, curiously, are most effective in increasingly *dilute* amounts, which is the opposite of what would be expected. Cures have been reported for medicines that are so dilute that not even a single molecule of the original medicine could remain. Also, in homeopathy, cures are usually more gradual and occur after some trial and error in prescribing medicines, in part because of the as-yet-not-understood dynamics of healing and because of the complex interplay of the medicines with other ingested substances and with the unique condition of a particular patient's body.

In my case, the doctor tried a single remedy on me called Trachlyte and that didn't seem to do any good. About six weeks later, I returned to his office and he gave me a homeopathic medicine "Sticta Pulmonaria" which I was to take at increasing dilutions on successive days. The doctor selected this particular remedy based on the electrical properties of my skin measured by a machine called a dermatron (reminiscent of Backster's apparatus). Interestingly, the symptoms gradually began to disappear, with more dramatic healing occurring when the dilution became very high. I am now almost fully recovered. Did the medicine help heal me? I do not know for sure, but I think that it probably had a significant effect.

Is there laboratory proof that a medicine can help to heal individuals in such great dilutions of water that not a single molecule of the original medicine remains? The answer to this question appears to be yes, according to carefully controlled "double blind" experiments by teams of researchers headed by the French immunologist Jacques Benveniste. Benveniste proposed that perhaps molecular information had somehow been imprinted in the water, which retained the memory of the medicine.

In the March/April 1989 issue of the *Yoga Journal,* writer Richard Leviton uses an apt outer-space metaphor to describe the results of the Benveniste team. "Like an astronaut," he writes, "peering beyond the membrane of Earth for a sudden glimpse of an unexpected horizon, Benveniste called the vista 'metamolecular biology' and left it at that." The origins, mysteries and potential of homeopathy are subjects covered in books such as *Homeopathy: Medicine for the 21st Century* by Dana Ullman, *Planet Medicine* by Richard Grossinger, and *Vibrational Medicine* by Richard Gerber.

Gerber, himself a traditionally trained M.D., puts forward an interesting model to explain homeopathy, acupuncture, and various unorthodox psychic and other anomalous energy healings. This model closely echoes my own attempts in this book to define our new science and reality. He proposes that we transcend the Newtonian model of Western allopathic medicines with "Einsteinian" medicine—one that incorporates the principles of quantum mechanics, indeterminancy, holography, energy fields, and consciousness. Again, we are reminded of the results and models of Backster, Sheldrake, Burr, Vogel and others that reflect the same basic principles underlying, or pointing to, the new reality.

Gerber sees the human as a "multidimensional being of energy and light, whose physical body is but a single component of a larger dynamic system." According to him, the interactions of subtle vibrations between an unseen essence of the body and that of an extremely-diluted or even non-physical homeopathic medicine could activate the healing process. In this model, administering strong allopathic medicines might be likened to using a sledge hammer to kill a flea on one's finger: the flea *and* the finger become destroyed. Instead, one can use some of the principles of the new reality (the cosmic dance of inner-outer space interaction and the power each of us has over our own reality) to transform our bodies.

The old medicine, with its reliance on quick-action drugs and surgery, seems to be reaching a point of diminishing returns anyway. While we can be grateful for what twentieth-century medicine does offer us, probably the most rapidly increasing benefit that we can now expect in the health field is a new kind of medicine, or medical practice, based on wellness, the patient's willingness to participate in the healing process, and the treatment of root causes rather than symptoms.

My Unorthodox Healing Experiences

Beyond the remarkable healings of my knee and cough, I have only begun to investigate the possible new-reality avenues to healing. I admit that it is difficult for me, as a scientist, to attempt to understand or analyze how these unusual approaches to curing disease can be successful or even physically possible. I stand in awe of these rather subjective inner-space approaches, and if you detect an uncharacteristic lack of objectivity in my discussion to follow, it is because I have had to drop any of my familiar scientific models and take the plunge into unfamiliar territory.

For example, I once went to an Indian medicine man, who had placed his hands on me in a way that felt exactly as if they went *inside* my body. This caused some discomfort, some noisy gurgling, and then apparent healing of abdominal problems I had. Is it possible somehow to paranormally place a *physical* hand inside someone's body, as in the much-reported cases of the Filipino "psychic surgeons"? On some occasions, during times of heightened awareness such as in meditation, Laurene and I have experienced the sensation of one of our hands or arms sinking into the other's body. These may all be cases of experiences that defy ordinary explanation but are nevertheless quite real.

I have healed myself or renewed my body through vigorous physical exercise, polarity and aura balances, acupressure, jin shin and reflexology treatments, massages, rebirthing and other healing practices. I have discovered only now, well into my life, that taking good care of my body, eating the right foods and visiting healers is worth the investment of money and time. I feel better than I have for decades, but when I lose the physical discipline, when I get into predominantly mental states such as writing, for example, my body temporarily loses some of its energy.

The Role of Emotions

I have also come to realize that healing our emotions is just as important as healing our bodies. The two appear to be interwoven, as Gerber and other "new scientist" physicians have been pointing out. I have also had my challenges in dealing with my emotions. Thanks to years of workshops and therapy, I am just now beginning to deal efficiently with these problems. What I have needed to do is acknowledge my mistakes of the past with a sense of humility, to feel love and forgiveness toward myself and others, and to move enthusiastically forward into a free and flowing life.

The best-selling author Louise Hay, yet another potentially terminal case who cured herself of cancer, has expressed how diseases in various parts of our bodies reflect corresponding emotional blocks. For example, according to her research, arteriosclerosis represents resistance and tension, cancer represents deep hurt, heart attacks represent squeezing the joy out of life in favor of money or position, knee and neck problems represent inflexibility, and bladder problems represent being angry or "pissed off." Decades ago, Edgar Cayce, the "sleeping prophet," famous for his thousands of accurate at-a-distance psychic diagnoses and prescriptions, provided strikingly similar correlations of emotional and bodily states. These relations may not seem to have much scientific basis, but they provide an interesting framework for beginning to understand the relationship between our bodies and our emotions.

If we look at emotions and at what in the traditional metaphysical literature is called thought-forms as some still-not understood forms of vibratory energy, we have a clearer view of the new medicine. We can then see our bodies as receivers of a life energy that constantly renews us. The energy bathes our cells, giving rise to the apparent life-field observed by Burr and Wilhelm Reich in the laboratory. According to this theory, the degree to which we keep our bodies open enough to be available to experience and facilitate the flow of energy is the degree we can become healthy. As part of this regimen, we also need to be careful of the effect of our man-made environmental energies upon our bodies and the effects of what we put into our bodies.

Dowsing seems a good technique to measure the life force present in and around a person. While a healthy person sending or receiving love will have an expanded field, an unhealthy or fearful person will have an intensely contracted field. I have measured this phenomenon many times. The extent of our energy fields seems to be diagnostic of how well we are.

The Chakra System

In Chapter 7, we discussed how the ley lines which criss-cross the terrestrial landscape may be conduits for as-yet-to-be understood Earth energies. We recall that these lines may have properties analogous to acupuncture meridians on the human body. Acupuncture is an ancient medicine of the Far East that involves releasing blocked energy by mean of needles or by applying pressure to effect a healing response. We have also seen that at certain critical locations along the ley lines there exist energy centers sometimes coinciding with the megalithic sites.

These energy centers have their analogues in the human body in the so-called chakra system, which can also be manipulated for healing purposes. The long-standing knowledge of the significance of the chakras, virtually unknown by Western scientists, has been recently revived by the American physician Brugh Joy. In the course of his traditional clinical practice, much to his surprise, Joy sensed with his hands radiant energy fields coming from various areas of his patient's bodies. Only later did he discover that the fields he measured corresponded to those of the chakras. "Chakra" is a Sanskrit word referring to energy wheels associated with the top of the head (crown chakra), middle forehead (third eye chakra), throat (throat chakra), middle chest (heart chakra) and three lower ones.

"The chakra system," stated Joy in his book *Joy's Way*, "is a real physical aspect of the body but very subtle in comparison to ordinary physical aspects. . . . I believe the energy fields reflect and influence the structure of the body and its organization into organ systems. I also suspect that the chakra system is a mechanism that interrelates the gross physical body and the subtle or etheric bodies . . . and acupuncture meridian system. . . . I believe there is but one basic energy operating in these interrelated systems and that the chakra system modulates and transduces that basic energy. The body splays this one primary energy into its component frequencies just as the prism splays light."

My own introduction to chakras came one day, suddenly and unexpectedly. About five years ago I was finishing an assisting job during an intensive five-day Insight transformational training in Santa Monica, California. John-Roger, the seminar facilitator, was about to give a closing seminar. I was feeling self-assured and vibrant, having completed a period of service and sharing a group energy. As I was standing by the doorway, I noticed a distinct presence on my forehead, as if someone were pushing on it. At first I thought it might be a headache, but it was actually quite pleasant.

I had never felt anything like it before. The sensation rapidly intensified until I felt what seemed to be a two-inch hole in my forehead throbbing and opening like the iris diaphragm of a camera lens. At the same time this was occurring, I experienced an awareness of increasing interconnectedness with John-Roger and with other individuals in the room. I was calm and confident.

It was later explained to me that this experience was the opening of my third eye. This chakra, according to the perennial philosophy, is associated with mental awareness. I have been blessed with this gift ever since. The lens opens and closes according to what seems to be my state of consciousness at the moment. As I'm writing this, I feel it as open and almost throbbing. When I am driving in heavy traffic I find it closed. I call this attribute my "Light meter". It sometimes feels like a laser beam or beacon emanating from my forehead, shedding light through me as the wisdom of the universe and as my own mental acuity. These are subjective experiences and interpretations that transcend my identity as a highly trained scientist and are extremely difficult to apply to traditional experimental analysis.

Gradually I am coming to feel my other chakras open and close, one by one. I experienced my heart chakra first opening on one occasion when I was with Laurene. It created a loving energy I never felt before. Ever since that time, I feel this chakra opening and closing according to my degree of compassion and emotional openness. The iris diaphragm, in the case of the heart chakra, seems to be about six inches wide and sometimes feels like a deep hole in my chest. Now I really know what is meant by the phrase "coming from the heart." I have also noticed my crown tingling at certain times and places, especially in Egypt and Sedona, Arizona—two sacred sites. These are real physical sensations occurring quite spontaneously and they seem unlikely to be only the psychosomatic wish-fulfillment of my expectations. Like Brugh Joy, I started experiencing my chakras before becoming aware of their existence, location or sensation, as described in the traditional Indian literature.

I have also noticed that, although I exercise my legs a great deal, from my stomach downward, my body is not energetically as active. According to Joy, this corresponds to a person who tends to be "spacey," mental, and disconnected at times from the outer reality system. This may describe me as well; although I am working on "grounding" myself to counterbalance it.

If, as Joy suggests, our chakra system modulates and transduces the basic life energy within us, one wonders what happens when the chakras become clear and the energy can flow. This can lead to the kundalini experience familiar to the Eastern mystics. The positive effects of this can be instant healing and enlightenment, but one needs to be careful that the energy doesn't become so overwhelming that it could cause the body to go into shock.

The notion that our minds and bodies contain mechanisms to control and step down the enormous amounts of potential energy available to us seems well-supported by many leading thinkers, researchers, and fellow "inner space astronauts." Just as the chakras are transducers of life-giving energy to our bodies, our brains may be reducing valves for the power of a universal mind posited by the perennial philosophy. Aldous Huxley wrote in *The Doors of Perception*, ". . . each one of us is potentially Mind at Large. . . . To make biological survival possible, Mind at Large has to be funnelled through the reducing value of the brain and nervous system. What comes out at the other end is a measly trickle of the kind of consciousness which will help us to stay alive on the surface of this particular planet."

Healing the Earth

Yet even with the tools we have inherited for our survival on Earth, that very survival is threatened by forces seemingly beyond our individual control: nuclear war and global pollution. Given the evidence presented in this book for a transcending order in the universe, it now seems as though we might be able to do what previously seemed to be impossible: to transform ourselves and our planet through individual and collective thought and intention. If a lunar astronaut could blot out the entire Earth with his thumb, is it not possible to blot out terrestrial ecocide by swift stokes of healing consciousness?

Just as many of us are out-of-touch with our bodies and with the harmony of the universe, together as a social organism we are out of touch with the planetary environment of which we are a part. While many of us may disagree with my assertion of our enormous potential to heal ourselves, we will certainly agree with the assertion that our planet needs healing.

It has almost become a cliche that we have the capacity to destroy ourselves and our environment many times over with nuclear, biological, and chemical weaponry—yet we are still building weapons at prodigious rates. We are injecting carbon dioxide and other pollutants into our atmosphere at such a rate that our climates appear to be headed irreversibly toward the intolerable heat of a runaway greenhouse effect. We are depleting ozone from the stratosphere which is exposing us more and more to the lethal ultraviolet rays of the Sun. We are obliterating the tropical forests of the world at the rate of more than one acre per second. We are destroying irreplaceable animal and plant species. We are running out of fossil-fuel resources. And we leave behind acid rain, undrinkable water, unbreathable air, unusable land, oil spills, polluted seashores, radioactive waste, nuclear meltdowns, and unswimmable bodies of water.

From the perspective of a planetary scientist, I can clearly see how many of the major natural systems of the Earth, which once were in harmony, are now rapidly deteriorating toward intolerable living conditions. As ecologist David Brower put it, "It's healing time on Earth. We are not inheriting the Earth from our fathers, we are borrowing it from our children."

How are we to heal our planet in the presence of such extensive public denial and private greed? It seems that, by analogy to the terminal human patient, the old medicine of band aids, drugs, and surgery are not adequate to turn the tide. As Peter Russell suggests in *The Global Brain*, we need to risk looking at Gaia as a superorganism and at the already proven healing powers of the new medicine. As a collective consciousness, what can we do to heal the planet that has given us our existence and our health as individuals?

We can begin to look inward. We can use the group mind to envision a peaceful, harmonious planet. We can let go of our fears that the prognosis is grim, that the outcome will be disastrous, and instead act as joyful transformational scientists opening ourselves to the energy of healing just as Norman Cousins did. We can create for ourselves a global psychokinesis, a mind-over-matter series of physical changes to heal the injured knee that is our entire world. But first we must stop being only angry or fearful about our sorry state of affairs, and begin to forgive ourselves and others, and to bathe ourselves with the inner light I wrote of earlier. By using the power of our inner space, we can radiate our loving worldwide and thereby transform the planet.

We can go beyond our reductionistic science and accept our new holistic science. We can learn how to understand our home planet just as our megalithic forebears were evidently able to do. We can learn to diagnose its illnesses and to take action with love and good humor. And we can heal ourselves and our separate political structures as we heal the planet.

"Perhaps we are ready to learn," said humanist Alan Cohen, "that we have the power to give ourselves the healing for which we have waited. It may very well be that the lesson of our age is that the capacity to heal ourselves, one another, and our planet, lies *within* us. . . . The healing of the Planet Earth will come, for indeed it *has* come within our hearts. This transformation is being accomplished not simply through talking about it, wishing for it, or waiting for it. The healing is coming through *living* it, and it is coming through people like you and me, people who believe that we are worthy of peace. . . . the governments of the world must follow suit."

I am replacing my diplomas on the wall with pictures taken with my Soviet and Japanese friends, reminding me that my true credentials are those of a world citizen and not just an academic scientist worthy only of my specialty. On my wall there is a photograph of me sitting, looking into the eyes of Vitaly Sevastyanov, a Soviet cosmonaut and a special friend, with whom I feel a connection of the heart rather than of the head. The picture constantly reminds me of what I am here to do. Although he knows very little English and I very little Russian, the loving brotherhood the two of us have exchanged on occasion over the past twelve years is worth a billion words. As citizen diplomats, we *all* count. The story of the hundredth monkey and the experimental proof of the power of the collective mind, show us that every individual, working together with other such individuals, can make a tremendous difference in healing and transforming the world.

As we have seen in the case of individuals, diseases can seem to miraculously disappear simply by our being willing to open a block to the flow of energy moving through us. The same principles apply to the Earth as a whole. As Laurene Johnson, herself a healer, put it: "Our sickness and our pain are gifts from the universe, prodding us to come into balance. This is part of the perfection of the moment."

Steps Toward Healing the Earth

I have often been asked, how can an individual help to heal the planet? Is the problem not so overwhelming that one person cannot make a difference? Or, conversely, if highly diluted homeopathic medicines have an influence on the healing of a human body, could not a highly diluted mixture of humans enfolded onto the membrane of our planetary biosphere have an effect on all of us? Could not a band of "peaceful warriors," like the hundred monkeys, instill in us a sense of transformed habits and thus eliminate war, pollution, hunger and poverty from the Earth?

I believe all these things are possible, once we begin to adopt and operate by the light of models of our new reality. I pointed out in Chapter 2 that for this to happen, we need to develop a social consciousness. We need to adapt many of our new personally learned transformational skills to a planetary scale and perhaps even a universal scale. As a scientist, I am often reluctant to counsel others on the subjective aspects of living, but in my speeches and seminars I am asked this question too often to ignore: what can I do to help in the planetary transformational process? I have attempted to answer the question with the following briefly stated steps. These are based on my own personal experience, and I hope that they may help each of us develop a greater new global and cosmic participation:

1. Transform yourself: Be involved in some of the healing activities listed in this chapter to unblock your body, mind, and emotions. Let go and allow the higher energy to move through you. Stop resisting and denying. Experience the cosmic dance. Go to healers (with discernment) and let them help you move through your physical ailments, your fears, angers and lethargy into a loving consciousness. *Feel* that you create your own reality. Allow yourself to develop good health and financial prosperity through your thoughts so you can free up more time to be of service to others. Katherine Ponder has some excellent books to help increase health and prosperity through positive thinking and actions. These techniques have produced phenomenal results for several individuals I know. Some of this may take awhile, so be patient!

2. Develop a Social Consciousness—By self-contemplation and discussion with others, find those ways in which you can help develop and actualize your vision for a better world. Review the problems I have identified in this chapter and in Chapter 2, and begin to develop solutions, both on the practical and transcendental levels. Meditate on your task and ask for divine guidance, if you feel that will help. Formulate an intention and develop a plan of action. Use your expertise wherever possible. For example, become a citizen diplomat and begin to network with Soviet counterparts in your field.

3. Put your Vision into Action: Go out and do the work. For example, travel to the Soviet Union and work on joint projects of mutual benefit. We need to remind ourselves that peace is more than the absence of war. It is also an enthusiastic action of love.

Conclusion

As we have seen in this chapter, our healing potential is enormous. For me to realize this, I have had to let go of some of my scientific preconceptions and accept a greater reality which works but is also very subjective in nature and therefore difficult to relate in concrete terms. Mind over matter, homeopathy, and psychic healing are very real practices that yield tangible healing, even though we do not yet have definitive models that explain how this can take place. We find we can sidestep the old band-aid solutions that only focus on problems and suppress symptoms. We can instead move forthrightly as individual bodies of apparently multi-dimensional energy and as a more-cooperative global energy body into a lasting cure. We sense there is a greater power from within, an "inner light" that can be tapped to provide the energy for us to do what we need to do, as transforming inner space affects the outer space of our bodies and the Earth. These convictions are based on recent scientific evidence as well as on time-honored mystical and religious practice.

An appropriate symbol of the changing times that is our self-transforming culture is Shirley MacLaine's recently issued video "Inner Workout," which demonstrates how to heal through the use of meditation and the opening of the chakras. We are discovering that our outer workouts, such as those popularized by Jane Fonda, are just part of the equation. We are truly experiencing a worldwide revolution in medicine and healing—and none too soon for our troubled times.

Bibliography

Borysenko, Joan, *Minding the Body, Mending the Mind*, Addison-Wesley, New York (1987).

Brower, David, speech to Dreaming the New Dream conference, San Francisco (1988).

Cohen, Alan, *The Healing of the Planet Earth*, self-published (1988).

Cousins, Norman, *Anatomy of an Illness*, Norton, New York (1979).

Cousins, Norman, *Human Options*, Norton, New York (1981).

Einstein, Albert, *Ideas and Opinions*, p. 38, Crown, New York (1982).

Fuller, John Grant, *Arigo: Surgeon of the Rusty Knife*, Crowell, New York (1974).

Gerber, Richard, *Vibrational Medicine*, Bear & Co. (1988).

Grossinger, Richard, *Planet Medicine*, North Atlantic Books, Berkeley, Calif., revised edition (1987).

Hay, Louise, *Heal Your Body*, Hay, Santa Monica, Calf. (1976).

Huxley, Aldous, *The Doors of Perception*, Harper & Row, New York (1954).

Jones, Susan Smith, *Choose to be Healthy*, Celestial Arts, Berkeley (1987)

Joy, W. Brugh, *Joy's Way*, Tarcher, Los Angeles (1979).

Joy, W. Brugh, *Healing With Body Energy*, Audio Renaissance Tapes, Los Angeles (1987).

Leviton, Richard, "Homeopathy," *Yoga Journal*, p.50, March/April 1989.

Millman, Dan, "Way of the Peaceful Warrior," J.P. Tarcher, Los Angeles (1980).

Murphy, Michael, "Dimensions of Healing" and interview, *Noetic Sciences Review*, Fall 1987.

O'Regan, Brendan, "Healing: Synergies of Mind/Body/Spirit," *Institute of Noetic Sciences Newsletter*, Spring 1986.

Orr, Leonard and Sondra Ray, *Rebirthing in the New Age*, Celestial Arts, Berkeley (1977).

Ponder, Katherine, *The Dynamic Laws of Healing*, DeVorss & Co., Marina del Rey, Calif. (1966).

Ponder, Katherine, *Open Your Mind to Prosperity*, DeVorss & Co., Marina del Rey, Calif. (1971).

Siegel, Bernie, *Love, Medicine and Miracles*, Harper & Row, New York (1986).

Siegel, Bernie, *Peace, Love and Healing*, Harper & Row, New York (1989).

Ullman, Dana, *Homeopathy: Medicine for the 21st Century*, North Atlantic Books, Berkeley, Calif. (1988).

11

UNITY IN THE NEW MILLENNIUM

It is precisely the despair of our times that convinces me that a renaissance is right around the corner.
—Matthew Fox, *The Coming of the Cosmic Christ*

At times I have prided myself on being a futurist, one who could extrapolate the trends of our technologies to supercomputers, genetic engineering, nanotechnology, asteroid mining, space colonies, star ships, artificial intelligence, and radio contact with possible extraterrestrial civilizations. But now I see that this view is far too limited. My radical personal experiences over the past decade, and the rapidly accelerating scientific evidence described in this book, inevitably point us in a totally different direction. That direction leads us back to the importance of our inner experience as stressed through the millennia by our greatest spiritual leaders, as well as by our poets and recent "inner space" explorers such as John Lilly.

We have seen that most major developments of physics in this century have involved elementary particles that are not really particles but are evidently packets of energy that interact with the observer and with one another in ways that we yet do not clearly understand. We have seen that the UFO phenomenon is so pervasive and complex that we can no longer ignore the data. We have observed features on Mars that defy mundane description. We have analyzed at physical measurements from the megalithic sites in England that show us Earth energies do exist and are related to celestial cycles. We have seen that our thoughts and emotions can be communicated to plants and to our own donated, at-a-distance white blood cells and that distance (and perhaps time as well) do not matter. We have seen that near-death experiences, altered states of consciousness, and reincarnation data all point to the possibility that we may survive physical death—that immortality may be the true condition of our consciousness, a truth we must have had once, before civilization, and lost.

As a species, we are once again becoming universal newborns, but our denial of the widening cracks in our cosmic eggs could be our downfall, our suffocation. History shows time and again that, as we make the transition to a new world view, the old order holds on out of fear and habit until it can hold on no longer.

As Thomas Kuhn put it in his classic book *The Structure of Scientific Revolutions*, "The reception of a new paradigm often necessitates a redefinition of the corresponding science. Some old problems may be relegated to another science or declared entirely 'unscientific'. Others that were previously non-existent or trivial may, with a new paradigm, become the very archetypes of significant scientific achievement."

In history, we see several parallels to what appears to be happening now. Without judging the motive of the individuals and groups involved, we see that denial of the new is widespread. Thus Galileo's contemporaries who were unwilling to even look through his telescope are parallelled today by hundreds of modern astronomers who are unwilling to look outside a conference building for possible UFOs that have been reported in the area. We can also recall that a committee of the French Academy in 1772 refused to believe that meteorites existed. Many of our contemporary skeptics groups debunk all paranormal phenomena, from firewalking to pyschokinesis, from anomalous healings to near-death experiences.

John Maddox is the editor of *Nature*, ranked as the world's foremost interdisciplinary science journal—a journal in which I have published several times. Yet Maddox has shown the scientific instincts of a medieval church cleric. He said, with facetious intent, that Rupert Sheldrake's book *The New Science of Life* was the best candidate for burning in years, but his joke on himself, like so many such jokes, merely exposed his true feelings. On another occasion, he appointed a committee of uninformed outsiders to discredit several teams of scientists under Jacques Benveniste who had published in *Nature* a peer-reviewed paper presenting evidence of the biological effectiveness for highly diluted solutions of a particular antibody, lending support to the principles of homeopathic medicine. Note, the purpose of the team, which included a scientifically uneducated magician, was not to test for possible new laws, but to debunk, and restore orthodoxy to the kingdom.

I believe we need to move beyond the point of such denial and debunking. We must admit humbly we are confronting phenomena whose scientific basis is not yet understood. The sooner we focus on the phenomena rather than pretending they don't exist, the sooner we will unlock some of the extraordinary riddles confronting us. It is time scientists got on with the new work, with or without the support of our peers and our institutions.

Questions and Speculations

I cannot finish this book without some speculations about what the future might hold. I believe that the experimental results of the new sciences, while only preliminary, are still solid enough to make some inferences. For instance, we now know that our minds can play a powerful role in changing our inner and outer space. We sense that other-dimensional phenomena and beings may be impinging on our level of reality. And we know that we are capable of experientially accessing altered states of consciousness that can lead us into not just internal image realms but corresponding alternate realities; thus, the brain/mind is not the can of business-as-usual meat that biologists and psychologists claim. We appear to perhaps even survive physical death. Do we have souls? Are we immortal? Are we alone in the universe? Can we travel to, or be visited by, other dimensions? Can we transform ourselves and the Earth?

These questions have been posed throughout the ages by many of the religions and occult belief systems of the world. But somehow, we got sidetracked. Many of our present religions and philosophies have become self-serving and narrowly focused. Our modern science has separated itself from religion and has almost become a religion unto itself. Then, in the act of creating specialties, the sciences became even more fragmented, until we seem to have ended up with a chaotic hodgepodge of a world in which most of the questions posed have become trivial, short-sighted, and overspecialized. We seem to be more interested in measuring the energy of electrons in the magnetosphere than measuring energy emanating from the Earth and from human beings. We seem to be more interested in finding out the rate of tick infestation than the rate of cancer remission from unorthodox healing practice. And we conduct trivial experiments on animals to make a minor point or proof of useless quantitative data that takes precedence over the living being and conscious entityness of a mouse or dog or rabbit. We can inflict suffering on the universe because we have become so far removed from what reality is. Because we don't take our lives seriously as experience, we don't take the planet seriously as environment, and we don't take the lives of other creatures seriously. We end up experimenting rather than experiencing.

The new realities of our inner-outer space interconnection seem to still be beyond the reach of most of us. Our ability to ask the most important cosmic questions appears to have been obfuscated by dogma, denial, and fear. I don't mean to suggest that this is deliberate or malicious. Rather, it may be a sign of our times, a clue that something new is coming.

When asked, "What is the most important question you can ask in life?", Albert Einstein answered, "Is the universe a friendly place or not?" This question, together with other questions regarding our own immortality, the existence of extraterrestrials, other dimensions and energies needs to be addressed by the new sciences. Perhaps our implicit fear of the answer is what keeps us from addressing it. And yet, the question of whether the universe is friendly transcends the Big Bang because the Big Bang, by itself, attempts to deny the problem by pretending it is all an accident, as though that will make us feel more comfortable or remove from us the responsibility for our lives, and deaths.

The new sciences are spiritual. By spiritual, I mean an energy whose essence pervades all levels of being. Regardless of one's religious beliefs, the questions stand on their own, awaiting answers from our inner experience. When enough of us have had these experiences—whether we call them paranormal or spiritual awakenings or healings—and we can relate them to those of others, they will become part of our emerging world view and we will have a new consensus reality. Yet in order to take part in this grand adventure into the unknown, we must suspend disbelief and be willing to enter into the experience. Only through a decade of struggling with the duality between rational science and a sense of mystical spiritualism together with its paranormal effects, have I begun to merge them into the fabric of my own new reality. Because I have been trained as a scientist, I often revisited my new realities with disbelief and my struggle has been long. However, it may not take all of you as long.

The Impact of History

Early recorded human history, beginning more than 5000 years ago with the extraordinary cultures of Egypt, Sumeria, and northwest Europe, reveals some of the greatest truths and mysteries of the human condition. Before our technological society emerged, with its enormous benefits as well as its destructiveness, most people throughout the world came to their truths through their mythologies and by reaching inside. The masters of the Far East had reached elevated states of consciousness and taught others their secrets. Ancient tribes throughout the world, through their rituals, apparently connected with and utilized the energies of the Earth.

The UFO phenomenon, implying the possible existence of extraterrestrials or other-dimensional beings, may have pervaded all of history: from the time of the mysterious dawning of new cultures, to the miracles of the Bible and Fatima, to the present-day contact experience of apparently many thousands of people. Religions and civilizations may suddenly have appeared as a result of the transcendental nature of our inner-outer space explorations as a species, only later to be cut down by human vanity and organizational anarchy or obstinacy.

When we remove some of the filters of our materialistic lives and quietly go inside and rewrite our history according to our cosmic identities, we will begin to answer the larger questions of our time. As Joseph Campbell, William Irwin Thompson, and others have repeatedly pointed out, the spiritually based myths of our history provide a common denominator for understanding who we are and why we are here. They have persisted on an unconscious and symbolic level for a long time not because they are mere vestiges but because they are truths to which we have no access any other way.

Reincarnation and Karma

According to the perennial philosophy, each of us has a purpose for incarnating on the Earth at this time. That part of us which is immortal and beyond space and time, sometimes known as the "soul", may be here to gain experience in these dimensions and learn lessons unlearned in previous lives.

The concept of a reincarnating soul may be difficult for some to accept. It seems to violate the precepts of many of our religions and virtually all of our science, education, government, and mass media in the West. And yet the evidence is abundant for this apparent truth, not as a laboratory experiment for us to repeat and prove, but as a possible reality to experience, one that gives us a framework for understanding our larger purpose.

In this view, our learning experiences on Earth play out the unwritten laws of cause and effect to which we are all subject. Some call this cosmic physics karma, an ancient Hindu concept that states a very complex version of the notion that what we put out, we will get back. We might reincarnate and experience our lives as a series of tests and growth events. We keep making the same mistakes again and again until we learn the lesson. Then we evolve to a higher level. According to this theory, the human soul survives physical death and, following a brief period of rest and review on a nonphysical level of reality, attaches itself to (or embodies itself within) a new body by means of which the learning and growing may continue. These ancient concepts appear to be newly validated by Ian Stevenson's research on children who have related verifiable stories of their past lives.

The implications are enormous: cause and effect appear to operate on a much larger scale than we had dreamed. Karma is apparently not a physical phenomenon like our Newtonian billiard balls predictably bouncing into one another. Rather, it seems to be an enormous cosmic dance in which every thought and action is mirrored back to us: if we love, we get it back. If we are fearful, we get that back. If we lock ourselves in rigid scientific cages, we create an environment of grand destruction.

It therefore follows that our minds and hearts may be so powerful we may eventually be able to create our own reality any time, any place. We have seen in this book scientific evidence to support this aspect of the new reality. We appear to inhabit a mirror world. Our single and collective minds on this planet seem to be reflecting to us a movement into either higher ground or into physical self-destruction personally and globally, depending on our own inner beliefs, emotions and expectations.

The stakes are very high now for us as a civilization, and we must move quickly into this broader view by way of widening the cracks in our cosmic eggs, or we may physically perish in the mess that is our own creation. We may need to return to the planet through countless reincarnations to clean up our mess—unless as individuals and collectively we can transform ourselves while we are still here. I agree with Buckminster Fuller: I believe we are running out of time, so it's now utopia or oblivion. We no longer have the luxuries of resisting our true nature by overskepticism and cultural fragmentation.

Unity

Because of our profound interconnectedness operating at levels beyond what is understood by our current sciences, and because we as individuals may well create our own reality, could the new reality also be true on a larger scale? Could we each be cells of a Gaia, which in turn is one of the cells of a larger universal consciousness or Being?

Interdisciplinary researcher and author Jon Klimo has provided us with a related metaphor: "Perhaps God, the Universe, or All-That-Exists, is really something like a dissociated Being, a multiple personality, as experienced from our perspective as Its own dissociated subpersonalities. All aspects of Creation are in an evolutionary process of overcoming this 'cosmological dissociation.' As part of this overcoming process, we are learning to transmute our condition of relative disconnectedness and to access ever more of the omniscience, omnipotence, omnipresence, and omnibenevolence of our common Universal Being. Unfortunately, at this stage of our evolution, much of the energy and information involved in such accessing is being condescendingly perceived as somehow sub-real or unreal, as only imaginational, delusional, mystical, magical, or paranormal in nature, whereas it is in actuality manifestations of a deeper truth and a greater reality."

I believe that the evidence in this book strongly supports such views as those whose truth quietly underlies our much more pervasive present illusion of a chaotic world reflected in the discourse of our daily lives.

"There is a unity in the universe and a unity in our own

experience," said Joseph Campbell. "We can no longer look for a spiritual order outside of our own experience."

Through our science and religion, we have separated ourselves from that cosmic unity. Our technological society is stumbling all over itself in diminishing returns and global pollution. Even our valiant efforts to explore outer space appear to be stymied by an overemphasis of the masculine principle, the yang of the sterile space stations and of Star Wars.

We have considered the hypothesis that our outer space is merely a reflection of our inner space and that this reflection is currently tarnished with illusion. We need to heal that inner space. We also need to reconnect with the vision of the whole Earth as seen from the Moon—a beautiful blue-green-white force-field. We must create a balance or we will fail as a species. We need the transcendent solutions of the new spiritual science rather than rehashings of the old and explaining away the awesome.

The Coming Second Copernican Revolution

In writing about the experience of firewalking, Willis Harman addressed the skeptics' denials of mind over matter: "The suggested 'explanations' that appear regularly in the media and scientific literature are much like adding epicycles to the Ptolemaic model—they give comfort to the explainer but add little to our real understanding."

In other words, we appear to be in the midst of a second Copernican revolution that is placing the power of our own inner space in the center of our personal solar systems. We are no longer the victims of an arbitrary material world; we *are* the masters, within the laws and limitations of karma. And we may even be able to transcend our karma with a loving consciousness. It is fashionable for some scientists to deny the reality of the revolution, to hang on to the old model, elaborating on it fragment by fragment until it becomes a hydra-headed, unmanageable beast. But we can no longer afford this. We can, and, I believe must, evolve to higher levels of consciousness if we are to transform the chaos of our times into a collective harmony that is necessary to our survival.

Science and Spirituality

Mystical teachings through the ages tell us we are far greater beings than we realize. "These things I do you shall do even greater," Jesus was reported to have said. We may have had to step down the brilliance of our being to accommodate to life here on Earth up until now. We seem to have forgotten about our magnificence. According to these perennial truths, we must explore and integrate both our inner and outer space in order to reveal to ourselves dimensions and realms that will enable us to reconnect to our true selves and to move quickly through our lessons here so we can evolve to higher states of awareness and learning.

How do we evolve? According to the teachers such as John-Roger we achieve those levels when we have balanced our karma on the lower levels through acts of loving, service, meditation, dedication to a higher purpose, and physical exercise and purification. Our coming transformation of ourselves and our planet perhaps brings with it an even higher reward: soul transcendence, free of the struggles of our present Earth-bound human condition. In this model, we come back here only by choice and to teach. If all this is true, our transcendence is no small prize.

Ironically, our very minds, which we are now discovering to be so powerful, also seem to present obstacles when it comes to accessing and evolving our souls. Our minds constantly chatter. That is why some people seek ways to silence the mind through meditation and inducing altered states. That is also perhaps why the instruments of the Dragon Project picked up a mysterious silence inside the Rollright stone circle. This may also explain my small transcendant experience inside the Newgrange burial chamber. Through silencing the environment, some of the ancient cultures may have known how to silence the mind and travel the inner and outer universes of indescribable wonder and beauty.

It is hard to do that now; for we are so distracted. Also it is difficult for younger people brought up in our materialist belief system to accept the greater reality of who we are. The limitations of our languages often provide a rigid social barrier to our enlightenment. Yet as Joseph Campbell so well stated it when he saw the picture of Earthrise taken by the Apollo astronauts over the lunar horizon: "Our ignorance and our complacency are coming to an end." The younger people, who have inherited this world and probably other worlds as well, have an enormous responsibility. The Yuppie approach to life will obviously not suffice.

Most of us disown our inner space because at some deep

level we somehow don't want to acknowledge its importance as a source of our reality. We feel like jittery astronauts on the launch pad having second thoughts about taking the journey. As Campbell put it, "The fear of the unknown, this free-fall into the future, can be detected all around us."

We have somehow convinced ourselves we have very little control over our inner *and* outer space. Our perception of our environment is that things appear to "happen" to us as if they were random events in a Newtonian universe. Yet we can change that perception by using our inner space to our advantage—whether it be by meditation, intuitions, therapy, workshops, retreats, or openness to altered states and other paranormal events. We have seen in this book the scientific grounds for suggesting that our inner space can profoundly influence our outer space. Two thousand years ago, Jesus told us that the kingdom of heaven lies within. Perhaps now we can *truly* create our own realities once we step out of the fatalistic, mechanistic view of the old science.

A Challenge to Scientists

I do not intend to totally invalidate three centuries of exploring our outer frontiers with Newtonian science. We have come a long way with it. But I believe that the time has arrived for scientists to begin to look at the universe from a new reality perspective. In my opinion, simple technical "fixes" of the outer environment will not be adequate to make the necessary changes to deal with the problems facing us here. Sooner or later, we will all need to dance the cosmic dance, to let go of our inhibitions and fears, to blend the inner and outer toward our inevitable transformation. I challenge my scientific colleagues to consider applying their analytical tools toward creating a sound theoretical and experimental basis for the new sciences and to develop the appropriate transformational technologies.

There is much work for us to do. We need to expand and further verify the experimental work on UFOs, Mars, the paranormal, and healing described in this book. We need to develop new theoretical models to explain the observations. And we need to engineer innovative solutions to our grave problems as well as to address our most fundamental metaphysical questions.

I believe that we are up to the task. I believe we can create an inner space Apollo program which would make use of the best and brightest scientific talent the world can offer. The resources are enormous: in the United States alone, over $50 billion in federal funds is spent each year on scientific and engineering research and development. Most of the money is now going toward conceiving weapons of massive destruction, developing controversial nuclear energy, and continuing a moribund outer space program. Virtually no public money is now allocated to the new sciences.

As American and planetary citizens, we can choose to change that. Only small fractions of our current federal research and development spending and manpower (say one-tenth) could go a long way in launching a major new international inner and outer space program. We can not only go to Mars with the Soviets and with other nations; together, we can truly begin to discover much more of who we are and what our planetary culture needs to do to transcend our difficulties. But we need visionary leadership to recognize the importance of these new priorities, so that our inner-outer space program can become more a part of everyday life. We need scientist-advocates to usher in the new reality for our culture.

I recently had a second dream following the one I described in the introduction. In that first dream, if you will recall, I had experienced a troubling communication gap between myself and a leading space scientist I once knew well, who lived in a gigantic Tudor house. He had had no interest in the new science I was doing. In the new dream, this individual invited me into his office, where he asked me to consider joining *his* team investigating the optical properties of light reflected off Mars. As this was the topic of my Berkeley Ph.D. thesis, I knew I could help. It was tempting for me to jump in and rejoin the team. There was the sense of security, of a fraternal belonging, of having continuity of funding for my work. But I hesitated about the offer: even though I knew the subject well, it wasn't of sufficient interest for me to pursue. If I accepted the offer I would still be pursuing the old agenda of reflected light from outer space and not the new agenda of radiated light from inner space. In the end, I needed to follow my heart, and so we parted cordially but sadly.

This second dream marks a major rite of passage for me. I discovered I needed to risk my own personal future on an uncertain collective future. I also discovered that our choice of which questions we ask lies at the core of innovative science. We need to be bold enough to ask new questions based on the anomalous observations and hypotheses of the new reality. Our task of deciding which questions to ask has barely begun.

Conclusion

I hope this book has demonstrated that we are now encountering a more profound order to things that includes both inner and outer realms of existence. We are *all* integral parts of this order. It is a far greater order than we have been led to believe by our science, by many of our religions, and by our humanities. We seem to be imbued with a life force and with minds to allow us to perform miracles. We are in a dynamic, conscious universe which is constantly unfolding with wonder, showing us the way to our greater reality. The choice is ours about whether or not we wish to embrace all this with open minds and hearts.

We can still maintain the discipline of our science while plumbing the depths and heights of our inner and outer space. Our science and our personal experience combine to give us a model of a self-organizing higher power without form guiding us through our lessons, through our adventures. When we tap into that power, we find that the whole is greater than the sum of the parts. Just as the gases hydrogen and oxygen combine to form water, just as a caterpillar becomes a butterfly, and just as our cells combine to form our miraculous bodies, we humans can also combine to form a greater reality of which we are only beginning to become aware. Applying the above analysis to our planet and universe, we see that we may be creating a substance or being totally unlike its former constituents. The derivative technologies from the new sciences will probably become very powerful and must therefore be used wisely.

I believe that the key to our collective synergism is to forgive the past, feel the perfection of the moment, suspend judgment, open our hearts, let go, and take our free fall into ourselves and the universe. No one knows what the future will hold, but it is clear that we are in the midst of an exciting revolution in thought, feeling, and intuition as we enter the new reality. The transformational sciences are telling us something unmistakable: there is a higher power guiding us from within and without. The cosmic choreography directing all of us is very elegant and sophisticated.

Some people call that higher power God.

Bibliography

Ash, David and Peter Hewitt, *Science of the Gods*, manuscript (1988).

Campbell, Joseph, interviewed by Eugene Kennedy, "Earthrise: The Dawning of a New Spiritual Awareness," *The New York Times Magazine*, April 15, 1979, pp 14-15.

Fox Matthew, *The Coming of the Cosmic Christ*, Harper & Row, New York (1988).

Harman, Willis, *Global Mind Change*, Knowledge Systems, Indianapolis, Indiana (1988).

John-Roger, *Passage into Spirit*, Baraka, Los Angeles (1984).

Johnson, Robert, *He*, Religious Publishing Company, King of Prussia, Penn. (1974).

Klimo, Jon, "Cosmological Dissociation: toward an understanding of how we create our own reality," *Proceedings of the Second International Conference on Paranormal Research*, Fort Collins, Colorado (1989).

Kuhn, Thomas, *The Structure of Scientific Revolutions*, University of Chicago Press (1970).

O'Regan, Brendan, "*Nature* vs. Nature: Science, Censorship and New Ideas," *Noetic Sciences Review*, Autumn 1988.

Pearce, Joseph Clinton, *The Crack in the Cosmic Egg*, Julian Press, New York (1971).

Rossner, John, *In Search of the Primordial Tradition and the Cosmic Christ*, p. 217-224, The Llewellyn New Times, St. Paul, Minnesota (1989).

Stevenson, Ian, "Reincarnation: Field Studies and Theoretical Issues," *Handbook of Parapsychology*, edit. Benjamin B. Wolman, Van Nostrand Reinhold Company, New York (1977).

Thompson, William Irwin, *The Time Falling Bodies Take to Light*, St. Martin's, New York, (1981).

Weber, Renee, *Dialogues with Scientists and Sages: The Search for Unity*, Routledge & Kegan Paul, London and New York (1986).

INDEX